4D
IMPACT

Olu Brown

4D IMPACT

Smash Barriers
Like a Smart Church

Abingdon Press
Nashville

4D IMPACT:
SMASH BARRIERS LIKE A SMART CHURCH

Copyright © 2019 by Abingdon Press

This book is printed on acid-free paper.

Library of Congress Cataloging-in-Publication Data has been requested.

978-1-5018-8022-3

Scripture quotations are taken from the Common English Bible, copyright 2011. Used by permission. All rights reserved.

19 20 21 22 23 24 25 26 27 28—10 9 8 7 6 5 4 3 2 1
MANUFACTURED IN THE UNITED STATES OF AMERICA

CONTENTS

Introduction

SMASHING BARRIERS

T
welve years ago, twenty-five of the greatest people in the world came together to start a new church named "Impact Church," which is a United Methodist congregation originally located in West End, Atlanta, Georgia. Now, twelve years later, Impact Church is one of the one hundred largest United Methodist churches in the United States out of more than thirty thousand United Methodist churches, and in 2016 Impact Church was named one of the fastest-growing new church starts in the United States. You can imagine that the past eleven years have been a super-fast journey, and our team has seen God's favor in mighty ways. Our motto—twelve years ago and to this very day—is Doing Church Differently™, and we were so excited and passionate about this motto that we actually had it trademarked. We smile every time a congregation uses the tagline. I have been blessed to serve as the founding and lead pastor of what one of those original twenty-five leaders called a "movement." Twelve years ago, we didn't set out to plant another United Methodist

church—we envisioned a movement. Over the past eleven years, I have learned a few things about church health and growth from my own experience as a church planter and from the many churches across the country that our team has supported and consulted with over the years. I have learned that the capital-*C* Church is filled with grace, and I've learned that hard work and sacrifice are necessary for a local church to be vital and growing. Serving in any church of any size requires a lot of work and sacrifice, but sometimes it's difficult for people on the outside of a growing and vital church to see what's going on underneath the successful surface. From the street view, it can be easy to make wrong assumptions and to overlook the intensity and consistency that characterizes a growing, vital church.

This book is for all churches and church leaders seeking to become vital and growing, or to remain vital and growing. This book may challenge you—I hope in a healthy way. It centers on four key principles for developing healthy and growing churches that smash barriers: Technology, Hospitality, Worship, and Systems. I am a living witness to these principles. As we say at Impact Church, you aren't called to lead an ordinary church; you are called to lead a movement.

The Church is one of the few organizations that has gotten a pass and has been allowed to live in the eighteenth century while the rest of the world has pushed into twenty-first-century systems, relationships, conversations, and structures. It can be argued that the Church gets a pass because it lives and exists by sacred books, theologies, and dogmas that must be kept in a certain era to help the world and people remain aligned on a moral axis. I understand this line of thought, but I am more inclined to hold the opposite opinion: if the Church does not step into the twenty-first century, the Church may become obsolete. To some this may seem an unhealthy commentary and observation to make since I serve the Church as a pastor and have been theologically trained. But it is my great love for the Church that has caused me to offer this pressing observation of the state of the Church in the United States.

Recently, in the United States, a major toy store named Toys "R" Us closed its doors. The retail chain was arguably the best in the business by convincing children that their selection of toys was the best and thus demanding that parents make trips to their locations for birthdays and Christmas. I never would have imagined one day walking past the doors of this famous toy store with my six-year-old son and seeing the word *Closed*. It was like my son and I were walking through the relics of the past while I told him stories about the good old days, explaining to him how this store used to be one of the few options a child in those days had to purchase quality and cutting-edge toys.

On second take, as I was talking to my son about the good old days, I realized the good old days weren't that long ago. Toys "R" Us had dominated the toy business just a decade ago and now was closing its doors. What obstacles did this company face that changed its trajectory? More important, what kept it from shattering the barrier and becoming an even more exceptional place for children and teens hoping to get the latest and the greatest toys and gadgets? In my curiosity and research to answer my question, I stumbled across a CNN Money article that revealed the two issues Toys "R" Us faced: debt and competition. The article mentioned that the company's mounting debt rendered it unable to make "the necessary investment in stores." The article went on to share a comment from the former CEO, David Brandon, about falling behind competition in the industry "on various fronts, including with regard to general upkeep and the condition of our stores."[1]

The toy industry, like many other businesses, organizations, and institutions, was shifting and changing. Big-box stores and online stores created tremendous competition, and any business without the resources to adapt and improve in order to meet and beat the competition would be pushed out of the market. That's what happened to my favorite childhood store. It was strange, staring at those shuttered doors with dismay, explaining to my six-year-old son what Toys "R" Us stores used to be and how dominant they were in the marketplace when I was a kid.

I wish I had a dollar for the number of times I have heard churches say they would do more in the community and invest more in missions if it wasn't for the high debt the church owed, or heard a church leader say, "If it wasn't for the other churches that have more dynamic youth experiences, our church would be soaring as well." All of these defenses may be fair and real to the complainer, but at the end of the day, they are excuses that will never change the reality of the local church unless the church leader decides to live in the future and not the past.

What does a failed toy store have to do with you and your church? Everything! It provides a good example of what our congregations are facing and, too often, how we are failing.

The purpose of this book is to help you lead your congregation to make critical shifts, so that it does not become a church that used to be. I hope to equip you to lead your congregation so that they actively reach people by developing vibrant programs to meet real needs of the people in your community. I hope to inspire you to create celebratory worship that transforms lives and hearts. It is my hope that this book helps you become a church that smashes the barriers in your path, a church that rejects the immobilizing weight of nostalgia for yesterday, a church that faces the competition of today and sees opportunity and a church full of hope. In the twenty-first-century US Church, we are in a fight to remain relevant and alive.

Sixty years ago the church's main source of competition was focusing on businesses opening on Sundays and community commerce functioning seven days a week instead of six days a week. The chatter surrounding such developments was deeply upsetting for many people; it seemed like the world was coming to an end, if such a blasphemous idea could even be entertained. Today, there are communities filled with children and adults who no longer remember, or are even aware, that much of our society formerly functioned on six days and that on the seventh day of the week you would be lucky to find any store or business open. The world has shifted for Christian communities, and many of our churches have gotten lost and no longer see a way to forge a productive future, or to reach people in this new world and new way of living. The competition we face today, unlike sixty years ago, isn't six-days-a-week operating communities, but 24/7 communities filled with the noise of retail, recreation, and retreat. None of these are necessarily negative in themselves, but they have gradually filled the space in once-quiet and predictable six-day-a-week communities with soccer games on Mother's Day, twenty-four-hour coffee shops, tee times that start at 8 a.m. on Sunday mornings, and the list goes on and on. Never in history have churches had to compete with so many activities available to their parishioners and potential parishioners on Sundays—and every other day—until this present age, and so many of our clergypersons and church leaders are ill-equipped to stand out in such a noisy society filled with so much competition.

You may fear, as I do, that years from now your grandchildren and great-grandchildren will pass by the church you gave your heart to, and your grandchildren will find themselves explaining what the church used to be. This scenario is not inevitable. With the resources in this book, your great-grandchildren can be the beneficiaries of a vibrant and healthy church that lives into the future.

There is hope. We are living in the greatest evangelistic season of our lifetime. There has never been a better time for us to rise above the noise of our society and offer the world another option filled with grace and peace. We can become the disrupters, throwing a wrench into the current, seemingly endless cycle of retail, recreation, and retreat on any day or time of the week. Jürgen Moltmann wrote in *The Gospel of Liberation*, "Theology must be critical toward a sleeping church and a torpid tradition. It must battle the idolatry of anxiety which is running our churches. . . . Its critique must therefore be a critique of hope for a better church."[2] This book is about practical principles for church health and growth, not theology. But the desired outcome is the same—hope for a better Church, committed to dismantling barriers that cause communities to suffer, schools to fail, businesses to be greedy, politicians to turn blind eyes to social evils, criminal justice systems to be unfair, and greater divides between those who have and those who do not. In order to be this kind of church, your church must operate in multiple dimensions—a smart church, a 4D church. Just as a smart home, smart car, or smartphone is wired for success, your church can also be wired for success as you focus on four key areas: technology, hospitality, worship, and systems. We will explore and explain these areas one at a time in the following pages.

Chapter 1

YOUR CHURCH'S 4D NEW NORMAL

Change

Someone once told me, "Every seven seconds the world shifts," and with the access to technology that connects people to global platforms in seconds, churches have to compete like never before for people's attention and loyalty. In addition, as the norms of culture shift, new languages, practices, and behaviors are being introduced into our world. Unfortunately, many of our churches are not organized to reach people in the twenty-first century. "New normal" is an expression that is tossed around quite a bit in our society and can be heard in motion pictures, C-suite offices, boardrooms, counseling sessions, and internal conversations with oneself after experiencing a challenge or breakdown. *Normal* is a word that means common, expected, or everyday, but when you add *new* it forms a phrase that is a bit of an oxymoron. In one sense, when things are normal, they are predictable. When you add "new" to the equation, it means normal has been disrupted and a new routine or way of life is being introduced. I believe this is why the person told me that "every seven seconds the world shifts," and if we are not sleeping through life, in essence, every seven seconds something challenges our normal and causes us to live a "new normal." One disturbing way we are seeing this play out in our society is with school shootings, causing students, parents, educators, and law enforcement to rethink basic assumptions about safety and security in our academic institutions. Schools are living a "new normal." In our professional and personal lives, we have come to realize that we can't avoid disruptions that create "new normal" experiences. Although we try to accept change and even lean into it, there are times when we mitigate against changes that are too extreme, rapid, or frequent. For some, this may challenge the scripture, "Jesus Christ is the same yesterday, today, and forever!" (Heb 13:8). But we can celebrate that as Christians the most consistent part of life is Christ, and the most inconsistent part of life is living. My paternal grandmother in my eyes was an awesome woman, whom I got to know toward the end of her life and the beginning of my life. She was always filled with wisdom, and, of course, a little stern correction. Now that she has passed, I am thankful I remember only the sweet moments of wisdom and not those God-help-me moments of correction that she sometimes gave me. Perhaps it was during one of her famous all-day cooking sessions as she was making a delicious pecan pie that she told my mother, "You plan too much." These words became faith and life shaping for me at an early age. My grandmother wasn't suggesting we should live as rebels and let whatever happens, happen; she was saying, "Don't be overwhelmed or discouraged when life doesn't always work out the way you hoped or planned." Even our best plans can change. This is certainly true of the Church.

As pastor of a local church, I have been on the front line of Church change for many years and have seen adjustments in certain traditions of the Church, such as attire, regular church attendance, memorization of scripture, and financial generosity. At the same time I have seen an increase in new and expressive forms of worship, such as casual worship and small groups meeting in local office complexes during lunchtime. All of these experiences have helped me to see what so many of our denominational leaders fear that my grandmother saw so long ago: that we can plan for the future, but we should not be disappointed with what the future actually holds. I have seen great leaders build seminaries and churches with sweat, blood, and tears only to see in their lifetimes those seminaries fall into mediocrity and the local churches die on the vine. Many plans were made for communities, businesses, and schools to help usher in the grace of Christ, but something happened along the way and things shifted for many Christians in the United States of America. Some call it the Great Secularization of America. One article introduced a growing reality in America: "Americans—long known for their piety—were fleeing organized religion in increasing numbers. The vast majority still believed in God. But the share that rejected any religious affiliation was growing fast, rising from 6 percent in 1992 to 22 percent in 2014. Among Millennials, the figure was 35 percent."[1]

This growing secularism can be alarming to those who don't view the entire landscape of history and only view history through thin and predictable lenses. I don't choose to use the term "secular" in current culture because it creates a physical and spiritual disconnect between the secular and the sacred. I believe God created humanity to be both secular and sacred at the same time. We see this through the life of Christ who was both human and divine. Because we have this dichotomy within us and within our world, we can't be at war against one or the other. The "new normal" for the Church isn't being afraid of the rise of so-called secularism but seeing the age we are living in as a great opportunity to preach grace and help people see that God loves them and wants deeply to be in relationship with them. The *Atlantic* article illuminates the growing trend of people disconnecting from religion or not being attracted to religion, but it also shows a tremendous opportunity for church leaders who aren't afraid of this "new normal" to lean into and trust God for more.

Two of the many professions I admire and respect are engineering and construction. It is intriguing to see a person take raw earth and develop a house, building, hospital, or school. Years ago, one model of constructing new housing communities in suburbs was to buy a tract of land; carve out a hundred or so single-family homes; draw in a park, mailbox station, school, and a bank or two; and last but not least, a handful of faith communities. There was a time when construction developers sought out denominations to ensure that faith was expressed and tangible in new community developments. Today, times have changed and faith communities are no longer high priorities to developers. In our new normal, a church's physical property is more valuable than the church's prophetic voice and presence. Instead of seeking denominations to establish faith communities in new developments, developers are now buying older churches and demolishing them or converting them into lofts and condos. In my denomination (which has been in a steady decline for decades), we are seeing this happen at alarming rates. In some cases, we get a good financial return on the sale of church property, but this should set off alarms, in fact, because we aren't meant to be primarily in the real estate business. Our primary business—being a prophetic presence of God's grace and love—is being traded and sold on the auction blocks of twenty-first-century condo and loft developments.

While this reality may seem puzzling and dismal for some leaders, I believe we are living in an age of opportunity. God is reminding the Church of her value and challenging each of us to think differently about how we do and see church. As our church lives out Doing Church Differently™, we see it as a way of knowing and believing who we are in God in our world and how we have been called to function and exist today and tomorrow. Many church leaders are struggling because they identify more with a denomination, theology, and tradition than they do with Christ and whom Christ is calling them to be in this present age. If you want to be effective in the twenty-first century, reaching new people and reconnecting with existing people has to be a high priority. One of the most anti-evangelistic statements you can make is "I am a Baptist, Methodist, Pentecostal, or Catholic." These are labels, and there is more to each of us and more to our churches than the narrow categories our labels signify. You are a human being with unique gifts and graces that need to be shared with the world, and the same is true for your local church. I am not suggesting you should drop the denominational title from your church marquee, but I am saying that in the "new normal" we can't reach new people or reconnect with existing people by focusing on labels, which seem irrelevant to many people today. When we greet people with our denominational identity first—"Being a Methodist is the best way to know Christ" or "Presbyterians Rock"—they will run away and tune us out. The challenge we

5

face is not competition against secularism. It is waking up to a new way of doing church in order to reach people. Sounds new and old at the same time? Yes. And this is just the way God seems to move throughout history: as God introduces new revelations, God also affirms older traditions. God never gives us permission to stay where we are; God calls us to be sojourners on the way to the promised land, carrying with us those attributes and practices that are most significant and central to our faith.

This book is about traveling and moving toward God's destiny for our individual and collective spiritual lives and creating healthier, more vibrant churches. Identifying your church's 4D new normal is up to you as a leader. There is no easy way to discern how God is challenging your church and you as a leader to move and develop in this season. I have done some of the work by narrowing it down to these 4 Dimensions:

- technology

- hospitality

- worship

- systems

As you read the remaining chapters, think about yourself and your church not from your denominational or traditional taglines and mantras, but through the big idea of whom God is calling you to be in the twenty-first century. Think about your favorite sports team. For the sake of time, your favorite sports team is a football team. In the early days of football, the pros wore pigskin helmets and little to no body padding. You can easily argue those were the good old days and they needed less, but a human body will say a hard tackle is a hard tackle. Since pro football began, we have had so many advancements in playing field structure, lighting, uniforms, helmet design, and body padding. Basically, the sport of football hasn't changed, but how it is played has changed by leaps and bounds. The same must be true for your local church and how you lead your church and your willingness to refuse to allow things to be how they were and trust God for how they can be. Let's take this journey of new normal together, and as a guideline, and guardrail, I offer you 4 Dimensions that I think healthy and vital churches living in their new normal in the twenty-first century will use as guideposts and headline indicators. At the end of each chapter is a section titled Smart Church Reflection, consisting of three exercises: Reclaim, Rethink, and Regenerate. The chapters end with these guides to help lead you individually or your team through thinking processes about each dimension, and I hope you will examine the dimension in your setting and make necessary adjustments. I believe not only in you and your team but also that the best is yet to come in your ministry setting or local church.

Chapter 2

TECHNOLOGY

I was officiating a wedding at a church in Metro Atlanta, and while spending time with the groom and groomsmen not far from the sanctuary in a room that was the typical non-decorated afterthought space for groomsmen, I noticed a piece of dated technology on one of the tables. It was an old desktop computer that obviously no longer worked, and if it did, it was slower than a Model T Ford from the 1920s. Rarely do you see desktop computers anymore. Most have been replaced by laptops or smartphones, or at the very least, all-in-one desktops where the screen and hard drive are a single unit. This computer was a blast from the past, and although I was there to officiate a wedding, the desktop computer captured my attention. I immediately judged the entire church I was visiting and said to myself, "This church is so dated, it must be on the edge of becoming obsolete or extinct." I had never been to this church before, and after a first visit on a non-Sunday, and after seeing very little of the physical space, I made a snap judgment based on a single outdated computer. How many people visit churches and make similar judgments about their ministry, leadership, or relevance?

Perhaps my judgment wasn't too off base. A year or so after officiating at that wedding, the church was sold to developers and is now slated to become a new housing development.

How is it that a single piece of dated technology can show visitors looming signs of the nature of the church? A church's philosophy of technology is on display in every room, hallway, and corner, and tells a story whether the current leaders recognize it or not. It always strikes me as funny when a church leader announces to a congregation that the sanctuary is a place where all smartphones must be turned off. That would work ten years ago, but not now, when smartphone use is off the charts and is the way many people connect to the world. When we admonish people for using their smartphones, we are displaying our philosophy of technology—and it's an old, outdated philosophy. One recent article mentions the rise of smartphone use: "It's no secret that the modern day smartphones are overtaking the desktop's dominance as the primary gateway to the Internet and for media consumption."[1] So often, I see young adults and older adults in public spaces interacting more with their smartphones than with the people around them. As much as we say that people should be more intentional about verbal and social interactions, studies and quick scans of public places, like restaurants and malls, clearly show that asking people to disconnect from their smartphones is unlikely in our present-day culture. The reason I laugh whenever I hear church leaders telling people to discontinue use of their smartphones in church is because they are really saying, "Disconnect yourself from the entire world and resources to help you connect with God as we step back into the thirteenth century and bore you to death for a couple of hours." Sound crazy? It is, and this is what people who live in a technologically progressive world hear when they enter many churches for worship. I don't think we should ask people to choose between their technology or God. Rather, they should be invited to experience God through many of the devices they use on a daily basis whether that is to review scripture or fact-check the preacher on Google. Yes! Believe it or not, people are actually fact-checking you on Google as you preach. Technology is one point within the "4D New Normal" for local congregations as they face and embrace change. Those that lean in, intentionally developing a forward-looking philosophy of technology, will be the vital and healthy churches in the twenty-first century.

Whether we like it or not, technology is here to stay, and it can be one of the best ways to examine where we are socially and culturally as organizations and churches. When I think about the church of the twenty-first century, I think about churches that aren't second- or third-generation adaptors in the technology space but are leading the way and ensuring they support at every level the latest technology trends and developments. This doesn't mean churches need to become the next Google or Apple, but it does mean we don't need to fight the efforts of technology innovation, and we must find as many ways as possible to embrace technology in our church programs, administration, systems, and worship.

Trying to compete against the use and presence of technology in our local churches would be similar to a church leader attempting to stop the innovation of the Gutenberg press of the fifteenth century, which helped open the way for literature and Bibles to be shared with the masses as opposed to the few. Some might say that the revolution of the smartphone and other forms of technology from video, graphics, internet, and audio are modern-day Gutenberg press innovations that cannot be barricaded by a guardrail but must be released so information can flow to the masses.

Imagine the famous story in Matthew 14 when Jesus fed more than five thousand people with five loaves of bread and two fish. What if there was an app for that? The app may have helped optimize the logistics of feeding more than five thousand people with a few pieces of bread and fish? The app would direct Jesus and His disciples to the sectors where people received too much food and the sectors where people received too little food. It would have also told them how to store and package the leftovers from the miracle mass feeding. I believe Jesus would have embraced technology in such a way that would have enabled His disciples to fulfill the Great Commission found at the end of Matthew's Gospel. Oh! By the way, social media would have given Jesus and the disciples additional evangelism support after each miracle because people would have been following Him on Instagram and Twitter.

Consider the following technology philosophy: "Investing in the hardware and software resources that help communicate the gospel of Jesus Christ to the world is the right approach for a 4D Impact Smart Church." I offer this technology philosophy to help you develop your own philosophy. As I travel the country, coaching and talking to church leaders, I nearly always find a major gap in the church's use of technology. Striking a technology balance is not easy, but I hope your vision to fulfill the Great Commission aided by technology is not deterred by those who feel technology is not useful and doesn't have a place in the local church.

Now that the technology philosophy is set, the next step is to develop your technology approach and strategy. This is where you need to walk the fine line of negotiation and compromise. Leaders in the nonprofit sector and for-profit sector often ask different questions during technology discussions. In the nonprofit sector the technology discussion begins with "why?" In the for-profit sector, the technology discussion begins with "how much?" Nonprofit leaders have the hard task of convincing boards, elders, and laypersons about the "why" of technology, and this costs time and precious opportunities to reach new people for Jesus Christ. In the for-profit world, most leaders clearly realize the need (or the "why") for new and current technology to reach more customers and create more market share; their issue is often the affordability of the technology, not the value.

The leaders in your ministry should consistently understand and make decisions based on the philosophy of technology. That philosophy should be so evident to the people in your church that you are able to spend very little time on the "why" questions of technology and more time on the questions of "how much" and "what kind." It may take time to reach this point, but you should be working steadily toward it.

To assist your journey in establishing a strong technology emphasis in your local church or organization, let's focus on two types of technology categories: hardware and software. The hardware side of technology represents all of the real and tangible items used to warehouse and process technology systems. For example, a tablet, laptop, smartphone, flat-screen television, and phone system are all representative of technology hardware. The investment in current and reliable hardware is a must, and it gives an edge and resource to churches that want to remain relevant and current in our society and fulfill the Great Commission in Matthew 28:19 to reach new people for Jesus Christ. For instance, in the twelve-year journey of our local church, we've had to make consistent hardware technology investments that haven't always been easy or inexpensive. Much like your church, whenever we negotiate these investments, some of our leaders raise the question "why" instead of "how much." As a leader of a church/non-profit, I carry the extra burden of having to explain the why, but I have found that it is worth the process because more than 90 percent of the hardware technology investments that we have made over the years have been wise and necessary investments. One of the most recent hardware technology investments that we have made is switching from projection screens to LED screens. Although this investment was significant, it has reaped us benefits by providing greater graphic clarity for images and texts during worship experiences and increased rental of the facility.

At the close of each year, I review certain expenses, as I am sure you do as a leader in your local context. One expense I saw was for software technology that was not cheap and stood out as an outlier amid other expenses. The specific expense was for our church management software. If you are wondering what church management software is, it is technology that allows local churches to track visitors, giving, small groups, inventory, and even manage check-in stations for children and youth. It is a vital part of what helps our local church remain healthy, reach people for Jesus Christ, and connect them to each other. After reviewing the expense, I was able to answer the "why" for the expense and to justify the "how much," which is the cost. As you go through the process of developing your technology philosophy, when reviewing expenses my hope is that, when you have these moments, you will not make cuts or knee-jerk decisions without deeply understanding the "why" behind the technology investment.

The second category of technology is software, which includes applications, codes, and IT systems and allows individuals to use the hardware to communicate, design, text, illustrate, and create. Technology hardware and software are both necessary, and the designs and abilities of each change daily, and sometimes multiple times a day.

Before you go full speed ahead on technology hardware or software, let me tell you Ruth's story. As I was writing a portion of this chapter in a local restaurant that I frequent, I was blessed by a person named Ruth who asked me what I was doing. It turns out Ruth was an angel sent by God to help guide me in the course of writing this chapter. She helped me understand that churches can be too progressive with technology, leaving some people behind. I appreciate Ruth for her words of encouragement because I admit that I have often been so focused on the next technology that I forget many people in local churches haven't adopted the technology of now or yesterday, and we often fail to offer balance and blend. As you develop your technology philosophy, consider a balance and blend that will allow you to charge into the future with the latest and best while also helping those who may not embrace the latest and best to come along as well. Let's use the next part of the chapter to review some of the essential parts of your hardware and software systems in your local church.

Step 1: Technology Inventory

Reviewing your church's hardware and software systems sounds simple, but it is not as simple as you think because most churches have no idea of their current hardware/software inventory. The hardest part of this review is taking an hour or two out of a weekday to look through the entire church and write down all of the pieces of hardware and software the church uses or no longer uses. One type of technology hardware that may go unnoticed is the machine used to fold your worship bulletins. Although it doesn't have all the bells and whistles of a smartphone, it still needs to be counted in your technology hardware. Other overlooked technology hardware in local churches are media soundboards, microphones, and other audio equipment. Each of these are vital forms of technology that in some cases represent both technology hardware and software. Also, be sure to include inoperable technology on the list as well, such as phones from a previous phone system that weren't discarded.

Step 2: Review Your Technology Inventory List

Now that you have taken the time to list the inventory, what do you see? I am sure if you are like most churches, one of the first things you noticed is all of the hardware and software technology the church owns that you had no idea was still in the building or if it still worked. At the end of last year, our church updated our phone system. Guess what I saw in a box in the office? You guessed right, some of the old phones that we were no longer using. The question I raised was, "Why didn't someone throw these old phones away or give them away?" Sounds crazy, but we could make a comedy sketch about the technology you find in rooms and closets of churches that is never thrown away. I've wondered if there is an unspoken rule that when you get a new type of technology, you must hold on to the old technology as well, just in case. Now that you have uncovered your abundance of old and outdated technology hardware and software, immediately go to Step 3.

Step 3: Throw It Away

Most churches have a board or governing group that helps manage these types of decisions, and in a lot of cases, these groups make decisions very slowly or aren't familiar with the outdated or current technology hardware or software. Let me help you: circumvent the team and throw away the hardware or discontinue the software service as soon as possible. You will also find that you may be paying for software that the church is no longer using that is on a recurring payment to the vendor where the subscription needs to be canceled to save the church money and end wasteful spending. Remember, the vendor will not inform you that you are continuing to pay for a product you are no longer using. Have you ever subscribed to a particular app, perhaps an exercise app? The introductory deal was free for one month, then $10 per month with direct withdrawal payment. You initiated the contract because you wanted and needed to exercise more. The one-month free was an excellent deal, and $10 per month seemed to be pretty affordable. For the first two or three months, you used the app and workout plan religiously, but a few months later, you used the app less and less. The end result was that you continued paying $10 per month for a software technology that you no longer used and it was not in the best interest of the app developer/owner to tell you to end the contract and discontinue payments. This is a micro-example that you may experience personally, but on a macro level as a business or local church having several technology vendors and services that they are no longer using and continue to pay for can mean wasteful spending that is poor financial stewardship. In the case listed above, your personal budget may be impacted by a couple of a hundred dollars a year for unnecessary expenses, but for a local church or business, these unnecessary expenses can represent thousands of dollars that could have been used to fulfill the vision and mission of the organization.

Step 4: Make Tough Technology Decisions

With the inventory list in hand, review the manufacture dates for hardware and date of issue for the software. If upgrades to the hardware and software have not been made in five years or more, consider discontinuing or updating the hardware or software. As it relates to computers, using outdated hardware and software can cost the organization vital time and delay a staff person from doing an efficient and timely job. In some cases the church thinks it may be saving money by not updating technology when in reality the church is adding frustration to the staff forced to use the outdated technology and preventing them from doing timely and their best work. I am not urging you to use only the most cutting-edge technology, but it is vital to use technology that is current and offers the highest functionality you can afford, so that your technology actually helps you do the work of ministry more efficiently, equipping you to reach the world for Christ.

Now that you are empowered with these four steps, I hope you make wise hardware and software technology decisions in the future. You should complete this inventory every two to three years at a minimum. Now let's talk about technology consultants and budgets.

Technology Consultant(s)

You would think that as an author writing a book on technology suggestions for churches I would be some sort of technology expert, but the truth is, I am far from being an expert and need the help and support of experts. Whenever there is a technology question or need in your local church, one of your leaders or colleagues will always have a friend or family member who can help. Three out of ten times, this works out, and you ride off into the sunset with great advice and a superior technology investment. I didn't write this chapter for the three out of ten churches that hit the technology advice jackpot, but for the seven out of ten churches that experience advice disasters. When we initially started Impact Church in 2007, we had several technology experts who gave us advice, and it became confusing and felt as if we were going in circles with no destination in mind. We learned a hard lesson related to technology: "You will spend either time or money." Maybe I didn't mention that we were always trying to save money, and the advice we received was free. Remember, the free consultant route isn't always the best. I remember when our team needed a more robust server for emails and digital files, and although companies were going to cloud systems where they purchased server space and uploaded their data, we figured (because a free advisor told us) that it would be in our better interest to purchase our own server rather than purchase space from a company that was in the server business. Smart? Not so much. We purchased this bulky server, and once we purchased it we realized we didn't have our own building and had no place to store the server. We put all of our bright minds together and said, "Why don't we store it at the home of one of our team members." We lugged the bulky server into the home of the team member, the first of several server technology disasters. In the end, purchasing our own server wasn't the best decision, and we could have purchased server space from the experts for the amount we spent on our own server—which we never used. In this case we were trying to save money but we ended up spending more money and a lot of time. Did I mention lugging servers is backbreaking work? They didn't teach Server 101 in seminary.

There are people who will give you technology advice for free, but they may not tell you that your free consultation is prioritized below their paying clients. As a result, they may leave you waiting for answers or information you need to move forward. Each minute you wait turns into an hour, and an hour into a day, and a day into a week, and a week into a month. I have had numerous experiences like this as a pastor, hoping and waiting like a kid up all night before the Disney World trip and sadly disappointed when the trip was delayed or even canceled. I appreciate the gift of free consulting, but I really love reasonably priced consultants who do their work on time, every time. In the for-profit world, taking six months for a critical investment is an eternity that comes at a cost and may put the company at a disadvantage with their closest competition. Similarly, there is a cost in the nonprofit world with delayed decisions. These delays can hurt the church's mission and vision in the broader community. One cost you might not think of is the negative shape that this "free but late" consultation practice places on your church's culture. It teaches future leaders that free is always better, even if it costs the church six months or more of lost progress. I am not saying that you should always turn down free technology consulting services, but there are times when paying for expert advice, even a limited amount of it, is in the best interest of your church.

I know funds are limited. And like our team, you will come up with great cost-saving ideas that seem awesome around a table at 2 a.m. after everyone has had several cups of coffee, but in practice the idea will cost you more time and money than you need to spend. Take the lesson I learned: If you aren't a technology expert, consult a respected, experienced technology expert—even if it costs you money—to get their wisdom and advice. It will be money and energy well spent.

Now that you are convinced that technology consulting is one of the best investments for your 4D church, let's move on to technology budget because the technology consultant's first question will be "What is your budget?"

Technology Budget

It is counterintuitive to end the chapter with budget talk when linear logic would recommend that I begin the chapter with budget conversations. While budget defines scope, it also limits vision and if inserted too soon in the conversation will stifle creativity and innovation. Try living a little on the wild side and being disruptive and dream before you place a price tag on how much your technology dreams cost. Although this may go against conventional wisdom, and may be a challenge for you and your team, dream big about technology and shop around *before* you finalize your budget. When our new church was preparing to purchase our first permanent property after worshipping in a middle school for a number of years, we retained a fantastic real estate agent who almost quit because we didn't take the conventional/linear investor route to first submit a budget. We wanted to dream and even see properties that were out of our range so we would truly imagine the possibilities, and not be limited to a few digits on an Excel spreadsheet. Although it caused us to have some uncomfortable conversations with our agent, it worked and paid off, and now we have a phenomenal building because we took an unconventional approach. By the way, when we moved into our new building, we didn't purchase our own big, bulky server for our new building, but we outsourced the server technology and now pay the experts to do what they do best, so we can do what we do best: fulfill the Great Commission.

I know it isn't easy, but try taking an unconventional approach to setting a technology budget, shop around, and dream a little first. Don't let your fellow leaders or consultants lock you and your team into a static number, leading you to regret it later. You may never be able to afford all the technology you dream of, but you will never achieve all you can with technology if you begin with a limited budget number.

I learned this lesson a few years ago when our church needed a particular technology we could not afford, and God sent an angel to close the financial gap. We were part of the cutting edge of seeing church worshippers' generosity shift from primarily using cash and checks to debit and credit cards. We dreamed of investing in a giving kiosk that would allow people to share their generosity on Sunday mornings through electronic giving stations.

We found kiosks that were affordable, but still way above what we had budgeted, which was zero. To accomplish our goal, we met with a donor over breakfast and shared our research and explained the need. To our surprise, the donor wrote a check for the entire amount of one kiosk, and today we have five kiosks. Currently, more than 60 percent of our income is digital and God has supplied our needs. This example is one of many that I hope will inspire you and your team to hold fast to your technology vision and not be locked into a budget and budget limitations.

I would advise developing a technology budget that represents the hopes and dreams of your church and, through the support of your consultant, determine if the church can afford the base model, upgraded version, or premium. In the end, you will get what you pay for and you will also get what you have faith for.

Technology is critical for 4D churches living in their new normal, and when we fail to invest in it we limit the number of people our local church will reach. We learned an important lesson with the giving kiosks investments, which allows us to raise more money to fund missions and outreach and to build God's kingdom on earth. Technology isn't only about people hearing our voices through songs and sermons but it is also about communities feeling our presence through missions and outreach.

I read somewhere recently that many millennials sleep with their smartphones nearby. Interestingly, I spent an evening with a few of my nephews and my niece in Houston shortly after reading this. As they were getting ready for bed, I went into the room of my eleven-year-old nephew—who, by the way, has his own smartphone—and was quite surprised to see his smartphone resting on his pillow not far from his head. Not to belabor the old adage, but "when I was growing up...." You can fill in the blank. When I was growing up, there was never a phone in our room until the great cordless phone entered the world. The article I read about millennials was right, and I was experiencing this phenomenon with my young nephews and niece. (One day, when they get older, I will tell them how I intervened on their behalf with their retired educator grandmother when she was about to gift them with the blessed green-and-gold-trimmed encyclopedia collection that their mother and uncles used when we were kids!) Technology is here to stay. Churches can't ignore the blessing of technology, even though it can sometimes seem like a curse.

The world we are living in has shifted and continues to shift with each passing generation to the point that everyone is trying to play catch-up and stay on top of the next, next, next, next. As a matter of fact, I think there will be a new job offered by companies in a few years called "next." The job description will be unknown and the requirements will be "willing to think about the future at all times." Sounds like a cool job. The challenge with most faith communities is they aren't thinking "now." To be honest, most still have committee meetings to determine if it is time to vote to move beyond the past. Depending on where you are with the technology spectrum, you are smiling or frowning right now; to help calm the anxiety of those with frowns, let me lay the groundwork that the technology dimension is not specifically about the hardware and the software of technology, but the philosophy of technology. It is impossible to go where one can't think, and my challenge for each of us is to think into the future and enable those who can and will to help us get there in our local faith communities.

In a fantastic work by Tony Morgan on church growth titled *The Unstuck Church*, Morgan writes, "The reality is that organizations, including churches, can get stuck in any season of the life cycle. That's why it's important to determine what season the organization is in. Then we can intentionally interrupt it. The necessary interruption will look different based on where the church is on its life cycle."[2] Our churches are in need of an interruption, specifically the interruption of technology that helps the Church connect people to Christ.

As a leader in the local church, I am having to practice what I preach about technology. Over the past few years, I have committed some grave technical mistakes, such as not keeping up with the pace of change occurring in hardware and software. Although I have an extreme appreciation for technology, I have not been able to keep up with all of the new gadgets, apps, and computer developments that seem to evolve every single day. It took a while for me as a leader to know that no matter how much time I spend chasing the next version of technology, I will never be able to stay on the edge of technology and have time to remain current. I realized my role, as one of the leaders of our faith community, is to make sure I empower those who have the ability, time, and expertise with the freedom and resources to do what they do naturally and professionally, and it has made all the difference.

So back to the millennials. There is another concept about millennials we must understand because many faith communities are struggling with attracting, engaging, and retaining young people. I often use two images when teaching technology philosophy in small and large groups. I place two images on a single screen. Image 1: An outdated 8-track tape. Image 2: A current iPhone. The 8-track tape represents the technology of the past and the iPhone represents the technology of the future. I ask for an unassuming young person to come to the stage or the front of the venue as if I am the host of a TV game show. I show two pictures side by side and ask the audience to be quiet, and, no matter what, don't answer out loud. I ask the young person to look at the pictures on the left and the right and tell me what the images are. It almost never fails that the young person has no idea what the 8-track tape is, but they can always identify the iPhone. In case you are wondering, an 8-track tape is a historic form of playing music (the tape held only eight songs, hence the name 8-track). After the laughing stops, then I get serious and say if your faith community's technology investment and philosophy is based on an 8-track tape philosophy, there are young people who don't know you exist. This is when people sober up and the three cups of coffee they just had suddenly kick in; I have their full attention. The purpose of this exercise is not to shame anyone, but it is designed to awaken them to the reality that the world is constantly changing. We have only one choice to make and that is to keep up with the world as it relates to technology. My desire for the Church is that one day we will surpass the world markets and be the leaders in technology development and not always be the ones waiting in the line to get the new version of next.

It is no longer a question of "if" a church should have technology but "what type and how much" technology. Some church leaders are afraid to have the "technology" talk, but it is absolutely necessary and relevant that churches are engaging in the discussion and the investment of technology. I know what it feels like to be in a place of discouragement and fear around technology investments, to believe our church can't make the move financially or philosophically. Some of the best decisions I have made as a leader have been technology decisions. When the decisions were made we didn't have enough money or full data to prove the investment would work, but we had faith in our team and the wisdom of our consultants, so we took a leap. People ask me, "What is the secret that makes Impact work?" I can often tell they are expecting answers related to theology or tradition, but what they receive from me is our tagline, Doing Church Differently™. In the remaining chapters you will hear a lot more about Doing Church Differently™, but one of the greatest images of Doing Church Differently™ is embracing technology from the very beginning. Every organization has sacred texts to reflect on to remind them of why they started. One of our sacred texts at Impact Church is the original vision statement document written in 2006. I crafted this thesis while serving as an associate pastor at a local church in Atlanta nearly fifteen years ago and let leaders and mentors across the country read and review it to make it better. One segment of the document is the "Technology Overview."

> The entire facility will be technologically driven, utilizing the most innovative telephone, Internet, video-television display, messaging systems, signage, and lighting technology available. The technology of the facility will be similar to the technology in "Smart Homes." The purpose of the technology is to allow the members and friends to have access to similar technology used in their homes and places of work. Additionally, this technology will assist the emerging and minimally staffed congregation reach more people during its infancy stages by marketing "who we are and what we do."[3]

It is hard to believe that these words were written one year before we launched our new church. Impact Church is alive and thriving in part because of our commitment to technology. There was a vision and philosophy for technology at the very beginning of Impact Church, and I believe it has made all the difference.

Smart Church Reflection

Reclaim

Today, reclaim the importance of technology in your local church and develop a technology philosophy that empowers your leaders and local church. Don't forget that technology will help you fulfill the Great Commission.

Rethink

This is your opportunity to Do Church Differently™ and live out a new pattern and possibility of technology. Remember companies like Amazon and Dyson that use and embrace technology to shape and change our world. Sometimes in order to rethink, you have to be willing to surround yourself with people outside of your bubble who think differently. Your church will never take the technology leap of faith unless it can first think differently about technology. Find a technology consultant to help your team. You may have to pay for the service, but it will be money and time well spent.

Regenerate

With your technology assessment and recommendations in tow, you are now empowered to go forth and make the right investments for your church's present and future. With the support of this book, wisdom from consultants, and acknowledgement of the frustration of outdated equipment, you now have a chance to make the right investments based on need, data, and costs.

Chapter 3

HOSPITALITY

O ne of my favorite authors, Henri Nouwen, in his work
With Open Hands, offered the following prayer of hospitality, "Give me a share in your compassion, dear
God..."[1] Henri Nouwen is one of those authors who forces reflection, and after reflection a deep desire to be the best image of God
on earth. This profound prayer begins and ends with humanity
and how all of humanity is loved by God and cared for by God,
even when humanity fails to care for one another. It is difficult
to love the politician who takes a side or position opposite from
yours. It is frustrating to see the traditions of someone from a different culture as valid and sacred when the traditions challenge
your way of life and ideals. It is painful when someone hurts us
or hurts someone we love and we are called to forgive them as
Christians. Perhaps this is why Nouwen closes the prayer with the
words, "Give me a share in your compassion, dear God..." This
compassion and love that Nouwen speaks of is the same compassion and love Paul speaks of in 1 Corinthians when he declared,
"Now faith, hope, and love remain—these three things—and the

greatest of these is love" (13:13). Love is the common denominator of our world, and it is love that causes the world to go round even when hate, bitterness, and all of the "-isms" seem to cover the shining rays of love. Love is the birth of the Church, and it is love that causes the Church to share God's hospitality. This is why I believe it brings pain to God's heart when the Church does not practice or reflect true hospitality.

Some churches believe they practice hospitality, but after a brief, unbiased check, these churches fail miserably at offering basic hospitality, such as smiling, greeting newcomers warmly, and providing directional signage and consistent accessibility for those with special needs. The danger in the church world is that as a church ages, the likelihood of the church becoming more insulated and offering less hospitality is more likely. Without constant care and concern in the hospitality department, there are no magical alarms that will go off, alerting leaders that the church's hospitality is lacking. This only happens when you check your email on Monday morning and read that an upset guest was mistreated by the usher team who was more concerned about the upcoming football game than they were about ensuring the guest found a seat in the worship area. For many churches, achieving the level of basic hospitality would be more than enough, but in the twenty-first-century world, the 4D Church's new normal is extreme hospitality, meaning "All People Are Welcome, All People Are Worthy, and All People Have a Place." Extreme hospitality is best illustrated by this a famous quotation attributed to speechmaker Carl Buehner: "[People] may forget what you said—but they will never forget how you made them feel."[2] Hospitality is all about how you make people feel when they are in your presence. As a pastor of a local church having the privilege of connecting directly or indirectly with people throughout the week during good and bad times in their lives, I am constantly reminded to remember how people feel when they are in my presence. If I weren't a pastor, how people feel would still be important to me because I am wired as an introvert and some of the most painful moments in my life are when I go into a space with a lot of people and I don't know anyone. I am always thankful for the angel in the room who sees me literally frightened on the inside and comes to my aid with small talk that rescues me from an embarrassing moment. Because I struggle with going to new places and meeting new people, my hospitality radar is always raised and I work very hard so that people don't feel unloved, untouched, or unappreciated in our local church. A question you may want to ask yourself from time to time is, "How do people feel when they are in my presence?" Do they feel uncomfortable and like a single number in the midst of millions of people or number one in the midst of millions of people? Extreme hospitality means we go the extra mile beyond general hospitality, and we ensure those in our immediate space feel welcome and loved at all times.

Today like never before we need extreme hospitality in the current political, social, and digital climate in which we live. There isn't a single day that passes that a young person isn't bullied on social media or politicians blast and take low blows at each other. It is so easy on social media to mistreat someone or cause an offense because the lack of face-to-face proximity creates an emotional and social disconnect leaving some to feel that poor digital behavior is acceptable. This means, in our world, we have to be even more open to practicing extreme hospitality with our neighbors and friends even though we may differ in race, religion, and creed.

Hospitality must be practiced more intentionally and more often in our society than ever before. We are seeing a growing trend with corporations hiring Chief Diversity Officers and creating the following positions: hospitality and operations director, hospitality project manager, and director of hospitality services. There is an entire marketplace for hospitality-related professions, and the industry is booming, and many young people are majoring in hospitality in college and going out into the work world with great careers. It is very common for members of a business community to attend hospitality training exercises that allow them to brush up on customer service skills and practices so that the brand of the company or organization is protected at all times. Although corporations constantly train employees in hospitality best practices, we know there are times when this does not go well. We can do quick Google searches for "customer mistreatment" and see the name of a huge company being sued or fighting a public trial because a customer was refused service by an employee or made to feel unworthy. We must not confuse "sensitivity training" with "hospitality" because sensitivity training and hospitality are slightly different. Sensitivity training is focused on helping an employee see another person's value and self-worth in a place of work or an organization ensuring that it doesn't discriminate against an employee or customer and cause that person to feel devalued. Sensitivity training is very important and a key practice to maintain excellent customer service. Hospitality is much broader and deeper. Hospitality is a heart issue. Since hospitality is rooted in love, it causes us to connect with the eternal love of God and share the love of God with the world. When we practice hospitality, we are sensitive to the needs and feelings of others. One can practice sensitivity and still dislike or discriminate against a person, but if we share true hospitality, it is impossible to show hospitality and hate or discriminate against a person at the same time.

Hospitality is a biblical practice that forces the heart to see the true value of people and love them deeply. We are called to be more than sensitive as Christians and the Christian Church; we are called to show hospitality. This becomes problematic even in the Church when someone is different or lives in a way that is in conflict with our personal values. In the book of Acts, the Church practiced and personified hospitality:

> The community of believers was one in heart and mind. None of them would say, "This is mine!" about any of their possessions, but held everything in common. The apostles continued to bear powerful witness to the resurrection of the Lord Jesus, and an abundance of grace was at work among them all. There were no needy persons among them. Those who owned properties or houses would sell them, bring the proceeds from the sales, and place them in the care and under the authority of the apostles. Then it was distributed to anyone who was in need. (Acts 4:32-35)

The early Church leaders practiced more than sensitivity; they were intentional in providing hospitality to those in need or experiencing the lows of life. The leaders of the early Church demonstrated an unwavering commitment to see those who were lost connected to a larger body of believers. Although many disagreements among the early believers are documented in the book of Acts, they were able to overcome their disagreement through hospitality and the love of Christ. The tradition of offering hospitality continued through each movement of the Church and is still a defining part of every local Christian church throughout the world today. This is not to say that the Church hasn't experienced moments along the way when hospitality was not shown to all of

God's children; but hopefully the scorecard in heaven will show we had more hospitality wins than losses. We can never forget the times when the Church didn't show up to offer hospitality at all. I am completing the writing of this book in the year of the fiftieth anniversary of the assassination of Dr. Martin Luther King Jr. When I review the history of Dr. King, and so many others who fought during the civil rights movement in the United States, I am appalled at the pain, dissension, and mayhem that many local church leaders caused or allowed. Our hearts also ache as news stories continue to pour out about the abuse at the hands of some of the Catholic priests toward children and the deep pain and the long-term damage that were inflicted. These are just two examples of how the Church has failed at offering hospitality and how in these moments the Church did not live out her design or call.

I am sure you have countless examples of ways the Church has missed the mark in offering hospitality. I think about the many people who were and still are made to feel unloved by the Church because of marriage choice, sexual orientation, family of origin, or education and financial status. I do believe that whenever the Church doesn't show true hospitality, it grieves the heart of God and causes the world to see a misrepresentation of the true and loving God we serve. If your church is not doing well in the hospitality department, commit today to doing a better heart job of letting all people know they matter to God and to your local church.

Jesus spoke of hospitality when he said, "Then they will reply, 'Lord, when did we see you hungry or thirsty or a stranger or naked or sick or in prison and didn't do anything to help you?' Then he will answer, 'I assure you that when you haven't done it for one of the least of these, you haven't done it for me'" (Matt 25:44-45). The words Jesus told to His disciples reminded them that what they did for any other person would have an eternal impact on the kingdom of God and on earth. These words are still true today and compel us to do all we can to remain connected to God's world through hospitality. We have a tendency to focus more on heaven than on the people we meet today. Remember the quote that we shared at the beginning of this chapter, "[People] may forget what you said—but they will never forget how you made them feel."

As a pastor I grapple with these words of wisdom often as I am forced on a daily basis to play on the field of life and weigh in on difficult family, the community, and organizational and denominational decisions that impact lives and offer hospitality regardless of how I feel about the person or situation. I quickly realized in my work that I don't live on an island as a leader, and the decisions I make or fail to make have a tremendous effect on the people and communities I serve and how I make people feel. As it relates to the church I pastor, it is a new, healthy, and vital church that exudes hospitality, but I am under no illusion that this will always be the case. God forbid in the years to come that our church ceases to exist and we are a footnote in some history book. I hope the way we lived and served in the present age will cause the words of service, peace, and love to be written positively about Impact Church and for those who remember the church to remember it well and how our church made them feel loved, welcomed, and secure.

Some people were won to Christianity because of how another person made them feel through hospitality, which is a testament to the fact that most people want to belong and want to feel loved. When I was a student in middle and high school, I never had a group or a crowd that I felt fully accepted me or that I felt comfortable with on a social level. One of the toughest times during the school day was lunch, and I had to walk into the lunch area with my tray and quickly scan the room for a place to sit. Even today, I almost break out in a cold sweat when I think about how uncomfortable I was in those years. I also get upset because people told me that it would get better after I graduated, but it didn't get better. There are times in my life when I still feel like that middle school student holding a lunch tray, looking for a place to sit in a crowd of onlookers. This is one of the reasons the ministry of hospitality is so central to the mission at Impact Church. I never want people to feel like I felt in middle and high school. That's my hospitality story, and I am sure you have one. Whatever it is, use it to help those around you feel loved and welcome.

We know that hospitality is key to the Church, but what does hospitality look like in the twenty-first-century faith community seeking to reach the world for Christ? In the United States and in other countries, we are engaging in heated debates about immigration and who belongs and who doesn't belong. I hold fast to the words from Emma Lazarus's poem "The New Colossus," written on the Statue of Liberty in New York City, "Give me your tired, your poor, Your huddled masses yearning to breathe free, The wretched refuse of your teeming shore. Send these, the homeless, tempest-tost to me, I lift my lamp beside the golden door!"[3] The United States has always been engaged in a vigorous debate around immigration, and I don't see the debate ceasing or becoming less passionate. But I do see the Church remaining engaged to show hospitality and to always lift the story of the baby born in a manger in Bethlehem because there was no room for Him in the inn. The narrative of Jesus and how He came into the world is the attitude Christians should take toward those who are marginalized or outsiders. Hospitality and love always win, which is why Jesus's ministry was so powerful and beneficial during His lifetime. Now, more than two thousand years later, disciples of Jesus Christ still win with hospitality and love. Each year, our key leaders at Impact develop strategies and tactics to achieve ministry "wins" for the upcoming year. More than the number of people being baptized or confirmed, rededicating their lives to Christ, or receiving salvation, *showing hospitality* is our number one metric and goal, our highest priority. The blessing of hospitality is that it can be practiced by volunteers and staff, and is the cheapest line item on your budget. But hospitality is one of the most difficult cultures to establish in a local church. It challenges us to cross lines, which makes us uncomfortable. It challenges us to step over, to stand on the side of the other person, to feel what they feel and see what they see. Therefore, hospitality in the twenty-first-century Church is above and beyond and always considering the other person as much as we consider ourselves.

In Brené Brown's marvelous work *Braving the Wilderness*, she grapples with the concept of how we dehumanize and rehuman-ize. She writes, "Because so many time-worn systems of power have placed certain people outside the realm of what we see as human, much of our work now is more a matter of 'rehumaniza-tion.' That starts in the same place dehumanizing starts—with words and images."[4] This effort of "rehumanization" is the task of hospitality. It is a difficult task, even for the Church, because of the great pain and apathy that exist in the hearts of women and men today. I believe the only reason people can malign and use damaging words towards others on social media, in political discourse, and in news media is because we have dehumanized people, cultures, and communities so much that we no longer see certain people and communities as reflections of God and God's greatest creations. In my own life, when I think negatively or speak negatively about a person, I have to pause and ask myself if I really view this person as a creation from God. Typically, if I mistreat someone, it is because I fail to see them as a worthy and beautifully fashioned being by God almighty. Dehumanizing people is very damaging, and as leaders we have to be careful that we and the churches we lead don't act out of unconscious bias and so practice the very acts of discrimination and isolation that we accuse others of practicing. I believe more churches could reach more people in their communities if they only believed everyone in the community was created by God and worthy of God's grace.

Now that you have been fairly indoctrinated to my perspective of hospitality, let me be clear that hospitality has to go to the next level in the twenty-first-century Church; it must go to an "extreme" level and become extreme hospitality. This form of hospitality is "next level," future thinking, and involves preparation, because organizations that think about the future are prepared for the future. The twenty-first-century faith community is facing a phenomenon that may cause it to be left behind or, even worse, become irrelevant. In a Barna research project titled "Six Reasons Young Christians Leave Church," the number five and six reasons were: "They wrestle with the exclusive nature of Christianity," and "The church feels unfriendly to those who doubt."[5] Howard Thurman, like Jesus, compels us to always side with the part of our being that dares to love and not hate, build and not destroy. These reasons are important and cannot be ignored any longer. Young people feeling the Church is exclusive and unfriendly are key headline indicators that the Church is headed down a path of extinction and irrelevance that may be difficult to turn around.

More and more once-vital churches are closing, and leaders are losing hope. Much like the Toys "R" Us stores that used to dominate the toy market, this trend is predictable. It can also be adjusted and even reversed, I believe. Extreme hospitality is at the core of a turnaround strategy.

The following are the fundamental parts of extreme hospitality.

All People Are Welcome

It is evident that some people in faith communities struggle with welcoming people, which is mind-blowing because if there is any space and place where all people should be welcome, it should be the local church. When I think about welcoming all people, I think about a startling statement by Dr. Martin L. King Jr. many years ago highlighting the segregated nature of the church. He said, "Unfortunately, most of the major denominations still practice segregation in local churches, hospitals, schools, and other church institutions. It is appalling that the most segregated hour of Christian America is eleven o'clock on Sunday morning, the same hour when many are standing to sing: 'In Christ There Is No East Nor West.'"[6]

Segregation is a form of anti-hospitality that grieves the heart of God and doesn't demonstrate grace. Segregation takes place for many different reasons, and most important, because of a conscious or unconscious decision to disqualify others before they have an opportunity to play on the field of life. Segregation plays on the worst fears of humanity and gives people ungodly permission to discount the value or worth of others without ever meeting them or giving them a chance. Jesus's ministry was all about qualification and inclusion, inviting all people into a deeper relationship with Him and all of humanity. Remember the powerful meeting with Jesus and the Samaritan woman at the well in John 4. There were several reasons Jesus should not have been meeting with her, and two of the most glaring were gender and ethnicity. Yet Jesus risked his brand, public image, and platform to demonstrate what could be the mantra of His ministry: "All People are Welcome." Howard Thurman in his work *Jesus and the Disinherited* commented, "Every expression of intolerance, every attitude of meanness, every statute that limits and degrades, gives further justification for life-negation on the part of the weak toward the strong. It makes possible for an individual to be life-affirming and life-negating at one and the same time."[7] Through the actions and wisdom of Jesus, we are called to always be our better selves, to offer compassion and inclusion to those who are like us and those who are not like us. This is a sign of strength. Whenever we act on our fears about others, we are weak and not strong. Churches that make it a habit to welcome all people are stronger and healthier than churches that are selective in who they accept and allow into their space. There are millions of people around the world who call themselves Christians but fail to live one of the most basic principles of the faith displayed through the life of Christ: accepting all people. Even Jesus's own disciples questioned His newfound friend in John 4:27, "Just then, Jesus' disciples arrived and were shocked that he was talking with a woman. But no one asked, 'What do you want?' or 'Why are you talking with her?'"

Although the disciples did not speak and question Jesus, I believe they placed a higher value on social practices and norms than on relationship and belonging. According to culture, Jesus was not supposed to have a conversation with the woman because of her questionable background. Her background check and family of origin were not clean enough for Jesus's disciples to give her a pass. Isn't it interesting how we can be so close to Jesus and so far from humanity at the same time? To be a disciple of Jesus means more than understanding scripture. It also means living scripture even when it goes against social norms and laws. The woman's background did not match the experience of Jesus's disciples, so they questioned the relationship Jesus was establishing with her and her community of Samaria.

To welcome all people you have to be fundamentally interested in relationship more than membership. One of the privileges a new church pastor has is the chance to insert ingredients into a church in the foundational years, as opposed to inheriting the culture and tradition of an existing church that is already prepackaged and most of the time filled with unsavory hospitality practices and norms. In the technology chapter, I referred to Impact Church's vision foundation documents, and it is important to refer to them again in this chapter on hospitality and specifically on welcoming all people. As our team planted our new church, we had to make a decision about membership. This is commonly used in mainline denominations to express what it means for a person to be committed to the local church. I will never downplay the importance of membership to a local church, but after evaluating the shift in culture, I realized people were more interested in helping people become members of local churches and not building deep and abiding relationships with them. The mission of the denomination I am a part of is "Making Disciples for the Transformation of the World." Though it is key and important to our denominational identity, I believe it is easy to get membership and discipleship confused. The only way to prevent confusion is to focus on relationship and not membership. When we constituted our church in 2009, we did not receive "members," and to this very day we don't receive members but instead we call these newly committed persons "Impactors," who are people who are committed to Christ as disciples. For our local church, we focus more on building relationships than we do on making people members. When we focus on relationship, we destroy the barriers of entry and become a more inclusive community that welcomes people into faith with Christ as developing and growing disciples. The path to welcoming all people begins with relationship, and through the power of relationship, hatred and segregation are destroyed and hospitality is shared.

Today many churches are struggling with inclusion and welcoming all people regardless of class, race, education, sexual orientation, age, or any "-ism" you can name. These same churches sing songs of grace while at the same time practice the anti-hospitality practices of segregation and exclusion. The word *segregationist* is a powerful word, and in the United States conjures images of the Deep South, slavery, Jim Crow, and outright hatred toward people of color. My mother was the youngest of three girls, born in the segregated South. She attended a segregated elementary and high school in the small Texas town where she was born. Although she is many years removed from her formative years in public school, the wounds of segregation and lack of hospitality still haunt her thoughts and memories to this day. Recently, my mother and I went to the home of a family member who attended the same elementary and high school as my mother in the small Texas town. Our light conversations shifted to a heavier conversation brought about by a painful memory both my mother and the family member held of their years in a segregated elementary school. They told me a story that caused painful emotions to well up in my soul and helped me to see how hospitality has even been withheld from the youngest in our society in times past and present. My mother and the family member attended an all-black elementary school, which was near a creosote plant. If you are not aware of what creosote is or how it is used, go to your nearest telephone pole/ power line made of wood and notice the black chemical placed on the wood to keep it from decaying. Although one of the purposes of the creosote was to preserve telephone poles, the creosote is a harmful chemical and can cause great damage to the human body. When I researched creosote after the conversation with my mother and family member, I found the following: "Creosote, and arsenicals, are ranked among the most potent cancer agents, promoters of birth defects and reproductive problems, and nervous system toxicants. They contain chemicals that in other contexts are labeled hazardous waste because of the dioxin, furans and hexachlorobenzene contaminants that are found in them."[8]

The family member mentioned that there was runoff from the plant in a ditch not far from their school, and to get to the school, the children had to jump the ditch that contained the hazardous waste. He also said if they were playing outside with a ball and the ball went into the hazardous waste ditch, the kids would pick up the ball and continue playing. He laughed as he said, "It is a blessing we didn't become ill from the hazardous waste that was around us." Although years later, my mother and family member were able to laugh about something that would be a class-action lawsuit today, I knew how painful this must have been for them and dehumanizing as they became older and realized the danger that segregation placed them in as children. Segregation not only hurts the one it is intended to harm but it also hurts the one who inflicts the pain because it diminishes all of society and the ability of all of our children to soar and be their best. I know for most, the image of segregation seems far-off, like the story my mother and family member shared, but segregation isn't as far away and distant as many of us may assume. According to the words of Dr. King shared previously, many faith communities are staunch segregationists every Sunday between the hours of 9 a.m. and 12 noon. Although this may be a shock or surprise, it is the painful truth of Christianity in the United States. It is not the reflection of John 4 or the inclusion for which Jesus lived and died. Our generation is called to be braver than the previous generations, to be better than the division and hatred of our past. We are more than our denominations, family origins, academic associations, and business connections. We are Christians, and this means that as part of God's family, *all* of our family members are equally important and have the right to be welcomed into God's house.

I hope you welcome all people in your faith community on Sunday mornings and through every event or program carrying your church's brand, because the Church must be the witness of Jesus's life on earth.

Although I didn't know the story my mother and family member told me about jumping the creosote ditch when we started our new church, I did hold hope in my heart that Impact Church would be a church for all people. Now almost twelve years later, this philosophy of extreme hospitality has been challenged over and over again. Yet we have held fast to the belief and practice that all people are welcome. In some metro cities, like Atlanta, organizations upholding LGBTQ rights publish information about accepting organizations and encourage those organizations to post images of their inclusive philosophy on doors to their buildings. A couple of times, I was asked if Impact wanted to be listed in one of these publications, and I said no. Not because I don't believe in inclusion for LGBTQ individuals, but because I believe inclusion is something you live through example and openness to all people. I am not knocking listings or public postings of inclusion, and I understand the purpose and need in some places, but at Impact, we aim to practice full inclusion, and feel that if we fail—if any person feels excluded here—no digital publication listing or entry door posting will help. Inclusion, in our local context, is about people's hearts. If they are barricaded and hardened, people will feel it in spite of signs posted saying they are welcome. Extreme hospitality and inclusion are in our DNA. LGBTQ individuals are always welcome at Impact Church.

This struggle of welcoming "all people" has become a systemic issue that blocks many faith communities from reaching all of God's children with the same grace God extended to them. Faith communities are a little different than corporations that go through a vision process to develop a product, and ultimately, through funds and time spent on research and development, craft a cutting-edge product to sell. This product is marketed to a target group and pushed through commercials, social media, and word of mouth until the potential receiver decides to invest in the product. The difference between the Christian faith community and the corporate community is having a resource called grace and knowing the goal and the vision of the church, found in Matthew 28:19: "Therefore, go and make disciples of all nations." The resource is clear and the mission is set that every Christian faith community must be about the business of reaching all people with the resource of grace through Jesus Christ. This resource cannot be reserved only for people with a certain income or education level, but is shared with the world.

I was told of a seminary professor commenting on the Great Commission who offered the following question, "What do you do when the world shows up?" My paraphrase of this thought-and soul-provoking question is "What do you do when the Bible actually works?" Today, the world is showing up at our doorsteps, websites, social media streams, recreation tournaments, programs, and outreach events, but much of the world does not feel welcome—particularly those who represent certain cultures, creeds, practices, and lifestyles. Would a single-parent father feel welcome in your faith community? Would a same-sex couple feel comfortable presenting their child for baptism, christening, or dedication in your faith community? Would persons with PhDs in chemistry or engineering find an open heart in your ministry or be sidelined because of their level of education? Would a special-needs youth be welcomed in your youth group program? John 4 and Matthew 28 remind us to always remember that all people are welcome in spite of how we may feel about them. One of the most powerful assets your church possesses is an ability to welcome people. It may be the least used asset in your church, as well.

All People Are Worthy

The next level of extreme hospitality is that all people are worthy. In the United Methodist denomination, we focus a lot on grace, but as I live out ministry and fellowship with other Christians, I find that grace sometimes is not applied equally, and worth is allotted based upon circumstance. This is unfortunate because the Bible speaks about grace very often. One of the most familiar passages on grace is Romans 3:23-24: "All have sinned and fall short of God's glory, but all are treated as righteous freely by his grace because of a ransom that was paid by Christ Jesus."

In our world, we focus constantly on metrics and outcomes. As a church pastor who lives in both the spiritual and operational side of the Church, I value grace and outcomes but have to be careful not to assign one's worthiness too closely to the metrics and the outcomes that they achieve or fail to achieve. I can sense the tension you are feeling after reading those words and how it is a fine line between performance and grace, and I do believe too often we give poor performance and lack of go-get-it-ness a pass in the Church. Unfortunately, this hurts our Christian witness and can prolong the fulfillment of the vision of a local church. So what do you do? First, you understand that "all people are worthy" and created in the image of God. Second, you celebrate people even when they don't measure up to your or their own expectations. Third, remember you are made of clay and the grace and forgiveness God has given you is the same grace and forgiveness God has given to others. Worth is not about the number of accomplishments we make. We are worthy when we are born and every time we take a breath, even when we, or those around us, don't believe we are worthy.

Back to metrics and outcomes, it would be a harmful world if we could not hold people accountable and were forced to give everyone a first-place trophy in spite of poor effort or lack of preparation. Outcomes and measurements are extremely important for our global society to function, and I fully and wholeheartedly embrace them and encourage them. But when it comes to worthiness through grace, this is an "input" that is not determined by performance, but a gift from God in the form of love and compassion through Jesus Christ. So if you are like me, you are conflicted right now because earlier you read that metrics matter, but now you are reading they don't matter. To clarify, I am really saying both. No matter how many metrics or measurements life and society imposes, we will never fully measure up and will always fall short. For some people, this explanation is just enough to give up on excellence and settle for the mediocrity in the middle, but for others is it just enough to inspire them to do their very best, and after having done all they can, to know that God's grace is sufficient.

We are worthy through grace not because of the outcome of failing to meet the goal, but because of the grace God gave us before we knew we even needed it. This is what John Wesley, the founder of the Methodist movement, called Prevenient Grace, grace that arrived before we knew we needed it.

The goal of this chapter is not that we all agree on grace and worthiness and sing "Kumbaya" but that we examine our hearts and the practices of our local faith communities and ask ourselves, Do we really see all of God's children as worthy through grace? If the honest answer is no, then you and your local faith community have some work to do and will likely struggle to become a healthy and vital 4D smart church.

We are worthy not because of what we have done or can do, but because of what God has already done for us through Christ. Although I am in my early forties, I have been fortunate to still be invited to speak at youth events and secretly wonder when they are going to stop inviting me because I am over forty. Out of all the gatherings I address in a given year, speaking to young people causes me the greatest anxiety and joy. Anxiety because as a forty-something, I am no longer current on the culture of youth and young adults, and I always say something that causes the crowd to laugh at me. Joy because there is no greater feeling than to see a young person who looks in a mirror every day and feels worthless and broken and after one of my talks comes up to me and is encouraged and reminded of their worth in God. This is one of the reasons why we started Impact Church, and one of the reasons we have a great heart for young people to this very day. I accepted my call to ministry when I was seventeen as a senior in high school, and I remember the dramatic moment. My paternal grandfather, Robert Wesley Tatum, whose middle name I share, had passed, and my family gave me the blessing of offering the eulogy. I remember as the eulogy came to a conclusion, I could hear an audible voice say, "I want to tell young people how to get to heaven." Although I had had many God moments that confirmed my ministry road in life before my grandfather's funeral, that was the most profound and declarative call moment up until that time. Now more than twenty years later, I am still being invited to speak to young people, and the only words I have to tell them are, "You are worthy and you are worth it." These are the words I have for you as you read this chapter, "You are worthy and you are worth it." Perhaps if you are a leader struggling to see someone's worth, it may be because you struggle to see your own worth and value in certain areas of your life or journey. Even the strongest among us have days when we look in the mirror and we see an image and a story that causes us to feel ashamed or unloved. In these moments, if we are not careful, if we do not rely on the love and support of others to help correct our negative self-talk, we will redirect the target externally. We will begin to see others as broken, unforgivable, and worthless, viewing people as objects and not as valuable human beings. This is, of course, extremely detrimental to the congregations we lead and to the Church, which is meant to be one of God's greatest representations of acceptance and love on earth. I feel sad when I think about the number of people who no longer consider the Church as an option because they were harmed or mistreated by those who represented God through the Church. I want them to know that these people who harmed them and made them feel "less than" were not God and did not represent God's heart.

In the twenty-first century, those of us who are connected to the Church can no longer expect people just to believe and receive the good news. We have to demonstrate the good news and show them that they are welcome and that they are worthy. So if you are sitting in a committee meeting with fellow leaders and someone raises the question, "Why don't people just come?" help your fellow leader know people will not just come to a place that may harm them or one of their loved ones. In The United Methodist Church, we practice Safe Sanctuaries, which is a philosophy and system to keep children safe and protected when they are in our care. This program is excellent, and I pray other denominations and independent faith communities would adopt similar programs. Although Safe Sanctuaries protects our children, we didn't account for the harm we cause to adults and their families through our failure to see all people as worthy. Is your church safe for all people, and does it see all people as worthy? How can the Church be safe for all people? Seeing people as worthy is Extreme Hospitality 101.

All People Have a Place

Once we get our welcome and worth in alignment, then we can always find a place for people. Whenever welcome and worth aren't aligned, people will never find a place in your faith community because the first place for them is not physical, but it is in your heart. Here is a question to ask yourself and your leaders, "Who has God given us a heart for?" It is important to have an answer because the place that you are offering first begins in your heart for the people God has called you to and then becomes a physical location long after the heart has fallen in love with them.

When I was serving as an associate pastor of evangelism and outreach at a local church before branching out as a church planter, God gave me a heart for a community near downtown Atlanta named the West End. It was and still is a vital community filled with proud people and a rich history. It is close to dynamic colleges and universities and awesome restaurants, and holds the richness of Atlanta history, but over time, parts of the community had fallen into disrepair and experienced a lack of investment and luster. God gave me a heart for the West End community and the people. Fast-forward a couple of years later, when our denomination gave me the opportunity to plant a church. When asked where the church would be located, you guessed right, the West End. People who have heard about Impact Church's journey often don't know that God burdened my heart for our initial start community years before we ever started. In this case, the community provided a place for the start of our new church, and to return the grace, our new church needed to offer a place for the community in our hearts. Not only did God give us a heart for the community, God also gave us the heart for Brown Middle School, which was the first location for our worship experiences. Our first worship experience was on Sunday, January 7, 2007, and the rain was falling on the outside but the atmosphere on the inside was joyful and filled with sunlight. We realized that the heart God had given us for the school was not limited to Sunday morning but caused us to support the teachers and students Monday through Friday. I remember during our first year as a new church start that didn't have many resources, we decided to give a tithe donation to the teachers and staff in the school. We asked the principal to give us the names of every teacher and staff person and we donated funds to each person in the form of a prepaid debit card. We did this act of kindness because we had a heart for the school. We did this also because educators are typically underpaid, and many utilize their own funds to support their students and classrooms. This act of kindness won many hearts to our ministry. Although your faith community's journey may be quite different from Impact's, there is a place that your faith community can offer to the world. That place is significant because people want to belong and connect. But discerning the what and where and why of that place begins with the heart.

A few years ago, I participated in a three-year cohort with a group of clergy friends. We set out on a mission to travel the United States in search of best practices around enhancing our public speaking abilities and developing "third places" within our faith communities. I am not so sure how we did on becoming better public speakers but we did learn a lot about third places. A third place in modern society is a place of recreation, activity, or gathering where people feel comfortable, as if they are among family and friends. A third place is not home or work. An example today is a local coffee shop. In my generation a common example was represented in the television show *Cheers*, "Where everybody knows your name."

The show's theme song hit the nail on the head when its lyricists wrote, "Sometimes you want to go where everybody knows your name."[9] This place, whether it is physical or emotional, is the embodiment of a third place. Although the third place concept is not new, it is experiencing a revival in modern culture, and people are longing to believe and belong—believe in the fact that the world is bigger than them and their current challenges, and belong to a group that is affirming and encouraging. Churches don't always see themselves as third places, but those who do gain great cultural capital in their communities because they become known as a place where people are welcome and can use their God-given talents to impact the world. Whenever churches don't offer their third-place support, people turn to other spaces in society, like sports venues, coffee shops, and even work, to believe and belong. It can be argued that the Church in the US had to offer themselves as third places eighty years ago because so many Americans lived in one-stoplight towns, and one of the few places for socialization and belonging was the local church. Today, people have so many choices of places to believe and belong that it is as if the Church is no longer necessary. The Church, if we are to fulfill our mission, has a responsibility to offer a third place and offer the unique grace of Christ to those seeking to believe and belong.

When our team had the opportunity to purchase and design our first worship and gathering space for Impact Church a few years ago, initially we spent a great deal of time talking to our architects about our vision and how we wanted to create a place and space that was multipurpose and that lived beyond Sunday morning. Our team realized that churches are some of the most beautiful examples of architecture and human craftsmanship on earth, but unfortunately many are only open one day a week, and the majority of the world never sees the inside beyond the church's stained glass windows. We wanted to be part of the center of our new community, not a one-day-a-week destination or landmark people used to give directions to those passing through the area. We knew our campus needed to be multipurpose but most important, a third place beyond Sunday morning for people to gather and experience God's grace. It gives me joy whenever I come to our campuses midweek, during the day or evening, and see cars and people and have no idea why the people are on the campus, but I know our team is providing a third place for community meetings, start-up vision casting sessions, or middle school graduations. We are currently in a capital campaign to complete phase two at our campus, and once complete, the model and philosophy of a third space will live throughout rooms that resemble Disney World that are used throughout the week for birthday parties and celebrations for children. We also plan to offer work stations that are open 24/7 with coffee, the latest technology, and the warmth of the Holy Spirit while some bright young mind is huddled in a corner space with a makeshift team of other bright minds developing the latest and greatest app. All of this will happen beyond Sunday morning and make Impact Church one of the latest models of churches offering third places.

When it comes to offering a place for all people in your local church, if you are like a lot of leaders, you are extremely focused on Sunday morning and providing space for people on Sundays only; you will tackle space for Monday through Saturday later. OK, I get it. So let's talk about providing a place for people on Sundays. The key is understanding that although Sunday is an actual day of the week, and your church is an actual physical space, the place you provide for people on Sundays is not simply physical space; it is also emotional space—providing a sense of "belonging."

True story: Our church campus is located in an industrial park. The church parking lot is accessed by two gates along a long road. There's a public transportation bus stop at one end of the road, near one of the access gates. If that gate is closed, a person riding public transportation will have to walk a long distance to the second entry. With big truck traffic and unpredictable weather, this becomes more than a stroll and isn't a good sign of hospitality. The gate closest to the public transportation stop was closed one Sunday. A gentleman who usually arrived by public transportation was forced to walk the longer distance that day. He approached me before church and mentioned his concern and disappointment. I said I would handle it. Unfortunately, I didn't handle it until I saw the gentleman the next Sunday, and it dawned on me how deeply important this situation was. It may at first seem fairly insignificant, more of an irritation than anything else. But I realized that we were failing to show extreme hospitality to a person. We had created a space for him, but he was being denied convenient access to it. He could actually see the "third place" where he knew he would find God's grace, but it was difficult for him to reach it. It must have felt like a slap in the face to him, to be forced to trudge down a long road, walking alongside his destination, in order to gain physical entry to the place where he had come to experience love and support.

The following Sunday I was happy to see that the closer entry point was open. And the gentleman continues to come to our church.

Some people may read this story and say, "Wow! Olu is making a big deal about a gate entry point; the person can just walk to the other entry gate. No big deal." But this would be missing the point. Please understand that it is a big deal because it is about access and belonging in a place that isn't just physical—it's also about access and belonging in the emotional sense. If people can't access your physical spaces easily, they may make an emotional leap and assume there are other, nonphysical spaces that they can't access. It is about more than just the physical, mechanical nature of an open gate in the right place. It is about understanding the emotional experience, and intentionally opening the right emotional space for people too.

Remember the conversation about membership versus relationship? If you dare to develop relationships with people, they will surprise you in how well they serve in the local church. It is all about how we view people and open our hearts to them and welcome them into our space. If you reviewed the bios of most of Jesus's disciples, you would not automatically assume that these individuals were fit for duty to carry the gospel into all the world and would be people that Jesus would welcome into His space or heart. Like most people, we would have overlooked many of the disciples and selected those with more polished résumés and background experiences that would hint to the ability of one day becoming apostles of Jesus Christ. But Jesus showed us how important it is to see beyond a person's current position to their future possibilities. This is the formula for understanding that all people have a "place." Since the word *place* is a noun in this instance, one would ultimately think of finding the right ministry, team, group, or committee in which a newcomer could serve. But the idea of "place" must transition from a noun to a verb and the action become the opportunity for people to live out their life's purpose and call through a local faith community while remaining connected to the world. This is a new and radical view of place, but it is necessary for the action of extreme hospitality. Therefore, the place you are offering someone on Sunday is an extension of their God-given purpose.

This is when being an usher becomes more than helping some-one find a seat in worship; it is receiving an opportunity to greet someone who may be having the worst day of their lives and help them see that God loves them and is caring for them even in this difficult time. It means the person serving in the children's ministry is doing more than checking in children; this person is meeting young people filled with purpose who one day, through the church's powerful Christian education program, will grow into a well-respected educator, business person, or global leader.

The reason it is hard to find places for people in ministry is because we are not quite settled on welcome and worth. Like worth through grace, you could easily argue that a person should be able to serve and share in any area, but this is not so. Place is very important, so much so we have to be very strategic in the placement of people in order that the witness of the local church and the purpose of the individual are always valued highest.

We are encouraged to welcome all people because they are worthy through God's grace, and the action of welcoming be-comes their service to humanity through God's grace. Therefore, we have welcome, worth, and place.

When we fail to reclaim hospitality and shift it to the level of "extreme hospitality," we literally walk away from the purpose and hope of the Church and leave it to corporate and for-profit structures to lead the way in demonstrating what the Church is most gifted to do and share with the world.

So what does "extreme hospitality" look like in your world? Let's go back to the seminary professor's question from Matthew 28 that was shared earlier in the chapter, "What do you do when the world shows up?" This question is powerful to the point of blowing you off your feet and totally transforming the way we see the world and do church. Most of us major in the sending part, which is mission, but minor in the receiving part, which is hospitality. What the world needs now is love. As beautifully stated by Stevie Wonder, "Love's in need of love today."[10]

I would simply add another phrase or two that would say, "What the world needs now is hospitality, hospitality, hospitality." Like love, hospitality makes the world go round, and as I look at the dismal statistics related to Church growth, I wonder if we are missing the hospitality piece by a large margin because it seems the world may not feel welcomed in our steeple churches, storefront churches, house churches, and churches in a school. Like Stevie said, "love's in need," and hospitality is in need as well. Every day when we turn on the news and see painful stories of war, murder, poverty, and distress, I wonder what the world would be like if we offered hospitality and not hatred first.

Now that we have settled on welcome, worth, and place, let's spend some time on the application side of extreme hospitality. I believe there are three specific areas of focus for the application of extreme hospitality in local churches:

- space hospitality,
- marketing hospitality, and
- worship hospitality.

Space Hospitality

The first type of hospitality, "space hospitality," is probably the most subtle and overlooked type of hospitality and will cause you to lose (or gain) new people to your local faith community or organization. "Space" is all about the physical plant: worship area, hallways, functional rooms, and restrooms. I love talking to architects and hearing how they think about space and the words they use to describe space. Perhaps this is a tool most architects learn in their coursework. When we were sitting with the architects designing our new space for our campus, the architects would oftentimes pause to explain and help us understand why a particular design or layout might not be in our best interest, usually by going to the nearest wall and sketching a thought that had been captured in our brainstorming conversations. For a moment or two, I wondered if I had gone into the wrong profession and if I would have loved the world of design more than vocational ministry. After pondering for a minute, I reaffirmed that I chose the right profession or at least the right profession chose me.

Many of our conversations with the architects were about how we would use space and not about where a particular wall or entry door would be located. In the industry, this is called a "program," which is the process of the client thinking through all of the weekly, monthly, and annual activities that take place on a church's campus so that the architect can help the client think through current and future use of space. We would also toss around examples of other best-in-class spaces from churches or businesses that utilized space well. These conversations with the architect caused me to think differently about space and design and how they function; they especially got me thinking through utilizing space as a form of evangelism and not seeing the space as a one-dimensional, isolated part of a larger group of parts. I believe twenty-first-century churches must be multidimensional spaces and engaging at the same time. I understand that only a small percentage of people in faith communities may ever get an opportunity to design a new space or redesign an existing space, and some of the readers of this book have inherited spaces that are most likely outdated and no longer fit the current vision or purpose of their local church. As a guest speaker at churches across the country, I have seen a lot of different types of spaces and have seen spaces that were so dismal that they were unbearable to sit in and other spaces that were so vibrant and exciting that I never wanted to leave. It is in the latter spaces that I realized buildings can be used as tools for invitation, gathering, and evangelism beyond Sunday mornings to create safe and secure places for people to grow in their purpose. One well-known pastor, Andy Stanley, told the story in his book *Next Generation Leader*, "Author and seminary professor Howard Hendricks was recently asked to assess the declining numbers at a certain church. After attending services, he met with the board and made this recommendation: 'Put a fence around it and charge admission so that people can come in and see how church was done in the 1950's.' In other words, face the facts: You are hopelessly behind."[11] The churches that are referred to in *Next Generation Leader* are museum churches, and I am sure you don't have a museum church, but if you aren't sure, a litmus test for museum churches is that they are single-dimensional spaces built to hold the items of the past in safe and secure places so that the congregation can tour and reflect on the past. Just as museums maintain spaces for relics of the past and rarely change space usage, churches can become the same operationally and spiritually. Whenever this happens, these churches cease to be cutting-edge and vibrant twenty-first-century churches. This doesn't mean that your church shouldn't capture and curate possessions of the past, but the entire space should not be dedicated to only curating and reflection.

One of the reality shows I like is dedicated to restaurant makeovers, and the host is pretty bossy and pushy but seems to be effective in helping the restaurant owner know that if changes don't take place, their beloved place of business will cease to exist. When I watch the show, I wonder why some of the owners are dismayed. At times, they have tears in their eyes because they had no idea how outdated their restaurant spaces were and that no matter how hard they worked, they were actually going against the purpose of their business: to reach new customers and serve existing customers very well. I now realize that whether it is a museum or a failing restaurant, both can serve as examples of how many current faith communities struggle to survive while delivering the greatest message in the world.

So here are the tough words and the suggestion that I must offer: When you walk into your local faith community or organization, do you ever take the opportunity to view it as if you were a first-time visitor or invite other people who are unfamiliar with your space to offer you feedback on your space? If the answer is no, you are missing a chance to develop extreme hospitality through your existing space. The most encouraging news is it will not likely take a general contractor, or hammer and nails, to make positive hospitality changes in your space. It will take only a few tweaks, and you will be on your way. Here are a few examples of space hospitality that, with a small budget and a few people, can be easily done.

Restrooms

One of the most frequented spaces in your building are the restrooms, but what happens when no one can find the restrooms? And even worse, when they do locate them, the sinks, toilets, or urinals are out of order and appear to have been out of order for some time? Many people would say it is a financial issue, but it is really a hospitality issue. Take a moment to ensure that your restroom signage is clearly posted and that it is easy for a first-time guest to find the nearest restroom. Enter the restroom as a first-time guest and check for cleanliness, and that all sinks, toilets, and soap and paper towel dispensers are working properly. Remember, if an individual visits your church three times and each time the same item in the restroom is malfunctioning, that person will make an overall judgment about your church, which in most cases won't be good.

We took our restroom hospitality a step further and added amenities such as mints, an electric shoe polisher, and even televisions over each of the urinals in the men's restroom. We are known as the church with televisions in the men's restroom, and you would not believe how such a small investment has benefited us with free word-of-mouth marketing that we could not have paid for. It also makes a statement to men that says we value them and don't expect them to step back into the thirteenth century when they attend church and can keep current with the latest sports game while at a place of worship. Sounds like an easy win to me.

Main Hallways/Corridors

Churches often have names for hallways and gathering areas, such as narthex, grand hall, or fellowship hall. There are times when the language we use for our spaces clearly places those who are new at a disadvantage. Imagine being a first-time visitor and new to church in general and hearing during the announcement time that the speaker wants people to immediately go to the narthex after church to sign up to be a youth helper. Suddenly, the opportunity to be a volunteer starts swirling through your head. You think to yourself, "I like youth and I like helping, I would be a perfect fit, but there is one problem. Not only am I new to your church but I am also new to attending any church and don't understand church language; therefore, I am embarrassed to ask anyone how to locate the narthex." You decide to do the only thing you know to do, which is to go home after church instead of trying to find the narthex and signing up to be a youth volunteer. This example may seem extreme, but it isn't, and it is why for-profit companies film several commercials for a single product to make sure that the right language and imagery are used to speak to the intended audience. Most churches are still using language that speaks to a particular culture or generation that is older or well versed in church culture and language, and so many great opportunities are lost because the audience isn't in the business of translating church language. As you tour your church this weekend and look at the naming of gathering spaces and how these spaces are announced verbally or digitally in your marketing material, ask yourself, "Are we forcing our supporters to interpret outdated language?" If the answer is yes, you have some work to do and the most difficult part of your work will be to help train your fellow leaders to think differently and to think from the viewpoint of an outsider and not an insider.

Beyond the naming of spaces like hallways, another suggestion is using the space and transforming it to a non-static space to help your local church evangelize or publicize an upcoming event. Imagine the church was doing a sermon series on construction to launch an upcoming capital campaign. Most churches would only appeal to the congregation with construction language and imagery once the congregant entered the sanctuary or auditorium. What if you placed shovels, dirt piles, and construction tape, and even hang cool construction-related imagery from the ceilings, in the hallways that lead to the worship area, if possible? Because people are sensory beings, you could even pump in a sound effect of the annoying, but lifesaving *beep, beep, beep* that a construction vehicle makes when backing up to notify people that heavy equipment is near. Remember, God has blessed you with space that you often take for granted and leave as static space that never changes or adjusts. If you are saying "this is a great idea, but we don't have the budget," this is when creativity and relationships come into place. When we were doing a construction series and didn't have the money to buy construction props, we reached out to a person in our congregation who works for a construction company. He was more than happy to donate the equipment.

We will talk about aesthetic design more in the worship chapter, but it is important that you see the development of static spaces into inviting spaces as a form of hospitality, especially if you are desiring to reach new people who want to be engaged and drawn into the space from the moment they enter your parking lot or building.

Entry and Exit

When a property ages, the signage ages as well, and one of those areas of signage is related to exit and entry signage. Are the exit and entry doors clearly visible in your space? Managing these spaces well is what architects and builders call "life safety," because we owe it to people to ensure their safety while they are inside of our buildings. At our church, we had a fire safety professional tour our property with our staff and volunteer leaders to help promote fire safety awareness in our building and to point out critical exit and entry areas for emergency situations. This was an eye-opening experience for our team. We also initiated our first fire drill on a Sunday because of the training and life safety awareness. Protecting people while they are in your building is one of the greatest forms of hospitality you can offer. Sadly, in a day and age when people are walking into churches and taking the lives of innocent people, we also have to offer hospitality by making sure our key volunteers and staff are trained in active shooter awareness.

Nursery and Children's Spaces

We live in a twenty-first-century society where people pay lots of money for "extreme" childcare to ensure that their children are safe. The expectation that parents have of those companies they pay to care for their children is the same expectation they have for organizations such as churches that are mostly run by volunteers. We do this first because we love all children and want them to grow and flourish, and second, because churches have to examine their children's areas and make sure they are twenty-first-century quality. In the United Methodist denomination, we use a policy called Safe Sanctuaries (www.uminsure.org/safe-sanctuaries) that empowers every local church to ensure all children are safe and secure in sacred spaces. We continue to hear the troubling news reports of young people who have been harmed while in the care of the Church, and these types of incidents can be prevented if every church would take an extra step in providing hospitality to children that keeps them protected and safe.

In addition to being protected and safe, we also owe it to our young people to offer quality and aesthetically pleasing spaces to grow and develop their Christian ethic. I was fortunate to be raised by a community of educators who were master teachers and went above and beyond the basic requirements in their classrooms to create aesthetically pleasing multisensory spaces in which young people could grow and be engaged. Perhaps when the aesthetics conversations surface in your church, the first thought is budget, and the first response is "We don't have it." Remember the solution we used to acquire construction equipment we could not afford for a sermon series? You can do the same to acquire aesthetically pleasing resources to decorate your children's spaces as a form of evangelism and hospitality. As we prepare to build more children's spaces at our local church, the code words we are using with children and their parents are *Disney World*. We believe our children deserve "Disney World," and we are developing these types of spaces on our campus to give them environments in which to grow and develop. Even if budget is an issue, at the very least you can do a current check of your children's spaces for general safety, cleanliness, outdated or dangerous toys, and static one-dimensional images on the walls that aren't mentally stimulating to the children.

In a day and age when many churches are struggling to reach children and youth, it is no surprise that these age groups are missing from some local churches because of the church's refusal to offer nursery and children's space hospitality. Children can feel when they are loved and if their needs were considered in the planning and programming process. One of the greatest resource investments a church can make is in the area for children and youth. The return on this investment will be healthy Christian adults who understand service and hospitality.

However, don't be discouraged if your current spaces for children and youth don't reflect Disney World; the most important ingredient is caring and loving all children. The rest will follow.

Marketing Hospitality

Whether you realize it or not, your church is in the marketing business. Marketing is a key driver for how we share the news about our local churches to keep current attendees engaged and reach new attendees. Marketing is an additional form of hospitality to offer to the world because the Church offers grace, hope, and forgiveness through Jesus Christ. Our churches are always marketing directly and indirectly whenever we invite someone to our upcoming choir Christmas concert or vacation Bible school, or to a series on financial planning. Sometimes we market via social media, Internet, newspaper, television commercials, and word of mouth. Out of all of the marketing your local church does, word of mouth is the cheapest and most widespread form of marketing in your resource bank. One of the things we quickly overlook after we craft our very appealing message is showing hospitality through marketing so all people will feel welcome. This doesn't mean you will reach all people, but you surely don't want to prevent anyone from attending or sharing in our wonderful experiences. One of the ways we stumble in this area is by not providing contextual, or as I would like to call it, "hopeful" pictures in our media material—ones that clearly show that all people from all backgrounds, abilities, and cultures are welcome whether this is the current reality for your church or not. You could say this is false advertising, but I say it is "hopeful" advertising where we are showing our hopeful future and not our homogenous present. I believe heaven must be a place with many variations of colors, races, and cultures. It is the reflection of Revelation 7:9: "After this I looked, and there was a great crowd that no one could number. They were from every nation, tribe, people, and language. They were standing before the throne and before the Lamb. They wore white robes and held palm branches in their hands." This image of heaven is an image that I want to see on earth, and I believe it saddens God's heart when this is not the reflection in the majority of our churches. There is a lot of data available showing how so many of our churches are facing this reality, and although this is not the purpose of this book, it is noteworthy to highlight the great divide that exists in many local churches around race, creed, and culture.

To help share marketing hospitality at Impact Church, we have conversations with our teams that help lead marketing initiatives, and we emphasize sharing images with those we are trying to reach in our local church to help all people feel welcome. Imagine having the opportunity to host a community event at your local church and sending out an announcement over social media with images and text. The goal of the event is to offer a free community celebration during the summer with rides, candy, food, and fun for all who live in the church's ten-mile radius, which happens to be a very diverse community. If the announcement doesn't reflect images of the diversity of the people in the community and is not worded so that all people feel welcome, the invitations for the event will fall short in reaching the target audience. After the event the church leaders will complain and say, "We attempted to reach new and different people, but the same people showed up to our event." The leaders won't take the time to analyze the marketing strategy for the event and will lead on assumptions instead of facts. If the leaders step back and review the marketing material that was sent, they will notice a big mistake: The material did not reflect images of the people they were trying to reach. Therefore, those diverse groups of individuals did not attend the event. Sometimes new and different people don't attend our churches because they aren't sure they are welcome. When our marketing material doesn't reflect them, it reinforces their assumptions.

Marketing is also a form of hospitality whenever we share hope to the world around us and use our words to support and not break down humanity. Whether you realize it or not, your church has a brand, and your church's brand is being marketed to the world. There are some churches that have a brand of hope and do a good job with sharing this hope throughout the world. There are other churches that have a brand of exclusion and do a good job of marketing this around the world. As a pastor, I teach our team "everything is marketing," and we have to be intentional to ensure Impact Church's brand makes all people feel welcome, whole, and filled with hope.

Take the next few weeks and examine your church's marketing hospitality threshold and make the necessary adjustment to ensure that new and different people are welcome and that the brand of your church is hope for the world through a resurrected savior named Jesus Christ. People hear and receive enough gloom and despair on a daily basis, and the worst thing they can hear is bad news from a church that professes good news.

Worship Hospitality

The final form of hospitality is worship hospitality, which is arguably the most important of the three mentioned in this chapter. There are two forms of worship hospitality to lift and examine: online and in person.

Online Worship Hospitality

Although many churches do not offer online or on-demand audio or video of their worship experiences, it is worth mentioning in this chapter since in the near future this will be one of the most dominant forms of worship in the world. Religious thought leader and change agent Carey Nieuwhof wrote an article listing seven "disruptive church trends," in which he listed the number one trend as "A Move Beyond Church in a Box." He said, "Future churches will have a building...they'll just reach far beyond it. You'll still need a facility, a broadcast location, a school or theater to rent—some space in which to meet. But you'll need to think way beyond it."[12]

The way these future churches are thinking beyond their walls is via online experiences that reach people and demographics far beyond their zip codes. If your church does not currently offer worship online live or on demand, I would suggest that you spend the next year having serious conversations with experts about helping your church leverage this platform. More and more churches across the country are using online worship to reach people beyond their current circle of influence and are seeing new people click the video link and join the online stream.

As online worship was breaking onto the horizon a decade or so ago, some church leaders were concerned that people would not come to the physical church and exclusively choose online. I don't believe their concerns were realized but those leaders weren't looking at the big picture. As a matter of fact, according to church attendance stats in the US, church attendance in physical locations has already been on the decline.

Although I support physical churches, I realize some people will always choose to watch online on their phone or tablet from the comfort of their couch or bed and not always be bothered by being in a physical building bumping shoulders or engaging in church talk with other parishioners on Sundays. It is also a great way for first-time visitors to check out your church without attending physically, but the number of people who currently choose to participate online versus in person is a minority. There are so many people who are not connected to the local church and will make a leap of faith if they can access the sacred space without stepping through the doors. When we started online worship at Impact Church, we didn't start with the full set of features because we could not afford the full package, and we didn't have the volunteers or infrastructure resources to broadcast video. At first, we offered only audio that was on demand and not live. This meant a person had to come to our website on Monday to listen to the Sunday morning worship experiences. Later we upgraded our capabilities so that individuals could be anywhere in the world and connect to Impact online video and join us in a live worship experience. Now, if they miss the worship opportunity on Sunday, they can watch on demand any day of the week. If you currently don't offer online worship, you may become discouraged when you meet with the experts and find out the price tag for the type of system you will need. But there is hope. Just remember that where you start online isn't where you will end. Take initial steps and as your income and operations grow, you will see growth in your online worship capabilities. Don't get frustrated. Keep moving forward and taking your church into the online future. As you develop your online worship platform, the same in-person worship hospitality protocol applies to online worship.

Here are the keys to great online worship hospitality:

Strong Internet Signal

There is nothing more frustrating than listening to your favorite song in worship when suddenly the screen freezes, or there is an opportunity to serve and the signal goes out before you receive all the information for volunteering. This frustrates the internal online church team, but most important, it frustrates your online viewers, and if it continues, the likelihood of high online attendance will plateau and decline. When we started Impact Church, we were located in a public school and did not have access to their high speed internet system. We had to creatively weave together a solution until we had our own building and had better internet connectivity. In the end, you will have to fake it until you make it, but if you offer online worship, do all you can to have a strong internet signal.

Opportunity to Engage the Audience

Whenever people are watching online, it is important to acknowledge them and engage them, and this can best happen through worship song leaders and those who are leading worship as worship facilitators or liturgists. It is important for worship leaders to say, "We welcome our online audience or congregation. And although you may not be able to stand, join with us in worship in your own way." Maybe the worship facilitator/liturgist says, "Thank you for joining us for worship in person and online today. Please know your presence is important." Sometimes when we are leading or directing worship, there is an online audience. We forget that the world is watching, and we have to be intentional about making online attendees feel welcome by showing love through hospitality.

Specials—Communion, Baptism, and Membership Intake

At Impact Church, we call communion, baptism, and membership intake "specials" because these are special times in the life of the church. These are also special times of celebration for regular attendees and first-time attendees. When you offer online worship, invite the online community to share in these special experiences. For example, during communion, you may ask the online viewer, "As you take communion symbolically…" or if it is not against your church's doctrine, you may invite online viewers to prepare their own communion elements and partake along with the in-person congregation. Baptisms and membership intake are specials that invite online attendees around the world to join in the celebration with their family and friends who are being baptized or becoming members of the church. Often family members aren't able to travel to be there for these special occasions for their loved ones. As you lead these particular experiences in your local church, remember the online family members by acknowledging them and inviting them to share in these special moments by extending their hands toward the screens or praying a prayer in unison with the in-person attendees. Make sure that the online attendees can see text or special readings; it is vital for their full participation.

Online Host Volunteers

Online hosts are critical to the success of an online worship experience if the intent is to grow attendance and discipleship, and to eventually become an online campus. In time, churches realize having the right verbiage and Internet connectivity for online participation isn't enough, and a next step is needed in which an online facilitator or host engages the online community throughout the experience and answers questions. In the for-profit world, this is called "customer service." In the Church world it is called "attendee hospitality." This type of hospitality makes all the difference for an in-person or online attendee to have a positive experience or a negative experience. To set your mind at ease, this is not a must to start or to have a successful online worship experience, but it is a great addition to have, and in most cases can be led by volunteers. The purpose of the online host is to monitor the online questions and communications and support the online attendees. For example, the audio on the online feed may be distorted and an online attendee sends a screen message to the online host to inform them of the problem. The online host immediately informs the church's audio team of the sound distortion and the adjustment is made immediately. The online attendee feels valued and hospitality has been offered.

Contextual and Relevant Illustrations and Examples

One of the final considerations to be conscious of during online worship is using contextual and relevant illustrations and examples. In most cases, these are low-hanging fruit that can be easily added or corrected. For instance, if I were preaching a sermon and mentioned a local retail chain that was contextual to my community, then the example would not be relevant to the global community watching online. In a case such as this, a better word choice would be to simply say "store" and not name the actual store brand because it may not be relevant to the online community and would perhaps create a communication disconnect. If you were born and raised in the United States, it is almost impossible to not to be United States–centric. This typically isn't an issue unless you are talking to a non–United States audience. In the US, we typically say, "I am from America" and fail to say "the United States of America" or "North America." Whenever we say we are from America, a global citizen may ask, "Do you mean South America or North America?" Or we may say, "Welcome to our worship experience. Please stand

and offer warm hospitality to the person in your row through a smile, hug, or greeting." This is great if I am in worship, but what about if I am home and watching worship from my tablet?

These are just a few examples, but, of course, there are many other examples illustrated in all areas and roles in worship; ultimately, we must be more aware of the people who are sharing with us and make sure they feel connected.

In-Person Worship Hospitality

Now let's focus on in-person worship hospitality. You may think to yourself, "Why not capture this in the worship by design chapter?" Great question, but in-person worship is captured in this chapter because it is important enough to be highlighted as a stand-alone section on worship hospitality. Hospitality is what is presented once people enter your parking lot and the building to worship God in your context, and this is one of the most overlooked forms of hospitality in local churches. We frequently take people and hospitality for granted. Yet it is crucial to returning visitors/guests and in helping your current congregation understand that hospitality in worship is key. As I am writing this part of the book, I am on an airplane, and while sitting in my three-seat row next to the aisle, the airline attendant politely asked me if I would be willing to sit in a middle seat in another section of the plane so that two passengers traveling together could sit together in my row. I instantly started feeling pressure because I struggle with claustrophobia, and I politely told the flight attendant no. Thankfully, my row mate sitting by the window did not have the same concern and willingly gave up his seat. This illustrates how we all have our comfort zones, and although we can't accommodate everyone, we have to be sensitive to their concerns, fears, and thoughts as it relates to our worship spaces and offering worship hospitality. For instance, how many times have we punished people who arrive to worship on time and select the best and most comfortable seating area only to be told to move over or stand up for people who were late arriving to worship? Maybe you've had a dynamic worship leader in front of the people leading an awesome worship set or choir director doing a dynamic job, and with an innocent heart they ask everyone to stand to sing a particular verse or song. The worship leader or choir director did not mean any ill intent by the request, but they didn't take into consideration that there might be some people in worship who may not be able to physically stand.

Here are a few in-person worship reminders and helpful hints for hospitality:

- Allow people to stand or sit during worship at their level of comfort. They came to worship a loving God, not to join a cult.

- You will never get the right level for sound amplification, and if you notice people are sitting farther back in the worship space or stuffing cotton in their ears, it may be a good time to talk to the audio team about adjusting sound volume.

- Understanding a group's culture is essential. Words and phrases that are printed or spoken need to be culturally sensitive and not offend worshippers.

- Try not to treat people unfairly who attend worship on time by asking them to move over for late arrivals. Logistically section off parts of the seating area, and open new areas when capacity is reached. This will allow the worship area to be filled strategically and not haphazardly.

- A lot can be said about the length of worship experiences, and I have found many churches can reduce their worship length by thirty to forty minutes by being more streamlined and prepared for worship. There is a lot of fluff or time mismanagement in worship that overtaxes your attendees and can prevent some churches from growing numerically.

Parking Lot

Before anyone enters your worship space, they meet your church in the parking lot. Therefore, depending on the size of your church and car traffic, having parking lot volunteers is a must. These individuals help guide traffic and become the first line of hospitality in your local church. Even if you don't have parking lot volunteers, go out of your way to make sure your church's parking lot has well-kept green spaces and concrete and asphalt surfaces at a high-quality standard. First impressions are vital in growing a healthy and vibrant church. Recently, I had a conversation with an attendee after church and she mentioned the importance of the parking lot experience and how it negatively impacts her focus in worship when it doesn't go well. As much as you work to have worship go well inside the building, don't hinder your efforts with poor hospitality outside.

Greeters

There are several names used for greeters in local churches, but one of the most common is "ushers," and this role is key to in-person worship hospitality. When we started Impact Church, we did not have many bells and whistles, but we definitely had greeters present on day one, and even to this very day. Greeters are what some churches call the "glue" that holds people together in community. Beyond the local church this concept has been adopted by retail chains and school systems. On my children's first day of school, it was heartwarming to see greeters welcome the new and returning students. Since it was my son's first day in the first grade, the greeters made all the difference and assured him that he was in the right place. My daughter was attending her first day in the eighth grade, and although she was a pro and very comfortable in the school environment, I believe the greeters helped her feel even more relaxed and assured. Remember, people want to feel like they belong and are connected.

Whether you are a greater in retail, school, or church, it is a blessing and a calling. For this reason, not everyone needs to be greeters because they will do more harm than good if they are not equipped to be a greeter. If you have greeters, encourage them and thank them often; if you don't have greeters, consider incorporating them into your church's organizational model in the near future.

Audio, Visual, and Lighting Needs

Once you enter a worship space for any age group, audio, visual, and lighting are important parts of the space and can help or hinder hospitality. Have you ever been to a church where there was poor lighting on the stage/pulpit and it was difficult to see the person leading worship? Or perhaps the church had sufficient lighting but for some reason they decided to leave the lighting at movie theater level? Have you ever attended a church where the microphones had a mind of their own and no one could ever fix the loud-pitch squeal or constant feedback? Or maybe the microphones did not work at all. I would never assume that your church has all the money in the world, because our church doesn't, and I know how difficult addressing this area can be, but it is vital as a form of hospitality to make sure the church's audio and lighting systems are working properly at all times. Since the highest attendance day for most churches is Sunday, and people likely come only that one day a week, an issue that continues each week may cause worshippers to wonder who is attending to the care and needs of the church Monday through Saturday. We constantly tell our teams, "If something is broken on Sunday, fix it by the following Sunday."

Regarding visual needs, this may differ depending on the church, but in most cases, churches will not have visual magnification, such as TV monitors, projectors, screens, and LED panels. If you have these applications, make sure bulbs are current and the size of the screen is the right scale for the room, and utilize technology as a supplement for worship with care. Don't jam every aspect of the worship experience on screens so that it looks like people are looking at a movie for an entire worship experience. Video projection should enhance worship, not become the object of worship. Excellent and well-kept audio, video, and lighting can be a great strength for your church and aid in sharing hospitality to your attendees. Remember, whether you are hosting online worship or in-person worship, hospitality is important, and the level of hospitality God is calling the church to practice is extreme hospitality.

Smart Church Reflection

Reclaim

Hospitality should be the hallmark of the church and is best demonstrated through the grace of God. Don't be afraid to be who you are as a church and as people. Every church has hospitality blockers, and you have to move them out of the way so the light of grace can shine through.

Rethink

Today, hospitality is extreme hospitality where God is calling on you and your leaders to go the extra mile and show people the love of Christ. Think of your church, outreach, and programs as an extension of Christ in a world in need of hope.

Regenerate

Since the world is shifting every seven seconds, the way you offer hospitality has to shift. Bring a few core leaders together and list the things you currently do as a church in the hospitality area and ask the question, "How can we regenerate this area of hospitality and make it extreme hospitality?" Once the question is answered, go for it and execute the plan.

Chapter 4

WORSHIP

lthough the previous chapter ended with a focus on worship hospitality, this chapter squarely focuses on designing worship and will help you develop worship experiences that are dynamic and engaging. When I was in seminary at the Interdenominational Theological Center in Atlanta, Georgia, great emphasis was placed on worship and the importance of worship by two of my professors, Dr. Lomax and Dr. Costen. They co-taught a worship class that was one of my most impactful experiences during my seminary journey. In the worship class they taught, I learned about the order of worship, how to celebrate and plan worship, and how to contextualize worship for the target audience. With my seminary experiences and countless other experiences attending worship at local churches across the United States, and personally leading worship, I realized a seismic shift happening in the area of worship design. Specifically, I saw a pivot away from hosting worship and toward designing worship. Designing worship means that we see the whole of worship and take every liberty to make suggestions and adjustments to ensure the congregation fully understands the purpose and theme of the particular worship experience they are attending. One of the key elements to being a smart 4D church and smashing barriers is designing worship that is dynamic and relevant. This type of worship inspires, informs, and instructs people through the power of the Holy Spirit, and isn't cookie-cutter worship, but worship by design. Churches have a great opportunity to design worship that takes attendees to a deeper understanding of God, self, and the world. The inspiration found in the book of Joel is relevant for church leaders today who dare to design worship: "After that I will pour out my spirit upon everyone; your sons and your daughters will prophesy, your old men will dream dreams, and your young men will see visions" (Joel 2:28). Worship by design is engineered and adjusted to help people connect with the presence of God and flow in the power of the Spirit referred to in the book of Joel.

When we are in tune with God, our communities, and our individual selves, we can distinguish between non-design worship and design worship.

Non-Design Worship

- lack of connection to the community
- template as starting point
- rigid and static
- non-response oriented

Design Worship

- connection to the community

- communal and spiritual starting point

- fluid and flexible

When I think about worship by design, I think about vacuum cleaners. Specifically, Dyson vacuum cleaners. It is funny that the Dyson vacuum cleaner brand is so popular that it isn't referred to as a product but as a "Dyson." People may ask, "Do you have a Dyson?" and not "Do you have a vacuum cleaner?" Dyson is a thriving innovation and manufacturing company in the United Kingdom that sells a high-end and high-performing portfolio of vacuum cleaners and other products. I like and admire Dyson for their advances in technology, their ability to sell common products at higher price points, and their commitment to creativity and innovation. From time to time, I watch a Dyson company video that shows their relentless commitment to design and innovation and why they are able to sell a common vacuum cleaner for a high price point. While reviewing the video online, I came across a fascinating quote from the founder of the company, James Dyson, that emphasizes his commitment to design, "At school I opted for arts, put off by all the formulae in science. There was nothing that combined the two like design engineering does. I only stumbled on engineering by accident and immediately decided what I wanted to do—make things that work better."[1] This statement and viewpoint is spectacular and even more spectacular when you think about how Dyson's primary and groundbreaking product is a vacuum. Their commitment to excellent design also helped to launch other successful product lines, such as hand

and hair dryers, air treatment systems, fans, and lights. Dyson is constantly innovating and designing, not haphazardly, but strategically and purposefully. Here is what the founder, James Dyson, said about designing with excellence and strategy: "Like everyone we get frustrated by products that don't work properly. As design engineers we do something about it. We're all about invention and improvement."[2] The vacuum cleaners are also modern-day works of art that do more than keep homes, businesses, and places of recreation clean. They are designed to attract attention and create conversation. The company's pursuit of design improvement and innovation has positioned it as a leader in their marketplace. I wish every company and organization placed this much value on getting better at what they do. If there is a place where we can achieve that goal, it is in the Church. However, based on the current metrics and outcomes, many faith communities have fallen into the trap of mediocrity and playing the "oldies but goodies" as congregants worship at the Temple of Nostalgia each Sunday. Author and former director of Lewis Center for Church Leadership Lovett Weems cautioned against being stuck in the past in an article titled "Leading between Memory and Vision." Weems said, "Church leaders stand today between a past that is gone and a future awaiting its consummation. God's leaders are deeply steeped in the memory of God's great acts in history, in one's denomination, and in one's congregation. At the same time, however, God has placed them in a present context that poses many challenges. In truth, this has always been the stance from which God's people lead. Biblical accounts of the Babylonian exile offer lessons to today's church leaders living in the tension between a confident past and the still-unfolding promise of God's future."[3] God has a future for our churches and we have a responsibility as leaders to help our churches celebrate the past but move forward into innovative and grace-filled futures. There is more in front of our churches than behind our churches. Since God has given you and your church a vision for the future, why not trust God and lead toward it?

The early Church in the book of Acts possessed a relentless desire to become better and reach more people through innovative ways. Acts 6:1-3 says:

> About that time, while the number of disciples continued to increase, a complaint arose. Greek-speaking disciples accused the Aramaic-speaking disciples because their widows were being overlooked in the daily food service. The Twelve called a meeting of all the disciples and said, "It isn't right for us to set aside proclamation of God's word in order to serve tables. Brothers and sisters, carefully choose seven well-respected men from among you. They must be well-respected and endowed by the Spirit with exceptional wisdom. We will put them in charge of this concern."

This is an example of the early Church leaders being committed to excellence and moving the mission of the Church forward. They empowered people with abilities to handle certain programs, and they focused on areas where they could add value and further the mission of the Church. Sounds a bit like Dyson. I was extremely fortunate to grow up in churches where leaders demanded excellent in worship and worked very hard to ensure that congregants experience well-thought-out and planned worship services that touched their hearts, souls, and minds.

I have kept a close watch on companies like Dyson and compared them to the progress and lack of progress in many churches and wondered why churches aren't always committed to the relentless pursuit of better, especially in the area of worship. I don't have all of the answers, but I believe it is encapsulated in these three areas: (1) clergy who are more committed to upholding the traditions of the Church and not exploring the broad space of what God is doing in the Church today and tomorrow; (2) laypeople or non-clergy people who are stuck in what they know or have always done and fear the unknown of trusting God for new and vital experiences of worship; and (3) Christian denominations that, with the best of intentions, created books of worship and protocol to solidify and perpetuate the institution without realizing some of these resources would trap and confine the denomination in a bit of a time warp and the worship of the past.

Through worship by design, vital and healthy congregations have learned how to celebrate the past, look to the future, and course correct in the present at the same time. This can be exhausting work, but the payoff is attracting new people who become disciples of Jesus Christ and retaining existing people who become more deeply committed Christians. Remember the Dyson story and their relentless pursuit to invent and create more dynamic products for their customers? What if the Church thought this way about worship? Before you shut me out and say the most famous and dangerous words in the Church world, "We can't do this at our church," read a little further as I make my point. Here are some recent statistics regarding church attendance in the United States: In 1990, 20.4 percent of the population attended an Orthodox Christian church on any given weekend. In 2000, that percentage dropped to 18.7 percent, and to 17.7 percent by 2004. Only 23 to 25 percent of Americans show up to church at least three out of every eight Sundays.[4]

Think about your church as a for-profit business that is absolutely dependent on customers coming into a store or viewing online and making a purchase. Although sales ebb and flow in every business, there are peak business seasons where the business sees the greatest number of customers. The same is true for churches, and for the majority of churches in the United States, the peak business day is Sunday. You would be surprised by the number of churches that barely prepare for their peak business day of the week and instead just wing it. I wrote this chapter because it breaks my heart as I travel and teach the concept of worship by design and see the state of worship in our churches. A large number of church leaders are tired of winging it on Sundays and want to do worship differently, but they do not know how or where to start. There are people in their congregations who want more, too, but are unsure what "more" looks like.

"More" is not some distant eschatological concept that is unable to be achieved. More is here and now. More is something you can envision and plan and create. So if you are a leader in a local church and you are frustrated, my word of encouragement to you is to take back your church's Sundays. Prepare for your biggest day of the week. You will see immediate results. Impact Church isn't perfect in preparing for Sundays, but our team is deeply committed to the effort, and we push our team members to be ready and prepared for the attendees on Sundays. We have a responsibility as leaders to be professionals and show the world that through grace, the Holy Spirit, and preparation, we can host worship experiences that please God and appeal to people.

What is worship by design? It is similar to the Dyson company model. It is a relentless pursuit to connect to God and connect others to God through worship. At first read, it sounds easy and clichéd, but if you take on this challenge, it will be one of the hardest challenges you will face as a leader in your local church.

There are several key areas to worship by design:

- language

- productization

- planning

- execution

- evaluation

I. Language

The first thing to note: if you currently call your worship a "service," stop. That is antiquated language, and doesn't make sense to people living in the twenty-first century who are surrounded by multisensory and well-produced events, gatherings, and performances that are designed to capture and keep their attention. A more accurate, relevant, and descriptive word is *experience*. We experience the presence of Almighty God in worship, and we send people out to serve. "Experience" is more than an hour-long series of movements and chants listed in bullet points on a church bulletin. Experience is physical, mental, emotional, and spiritual. It is the flow and presence of the Holy Spirit that allows us to see and do more than we could do on our own. Remember the early Church in Acts 4:31: "After they prayed, the place where they were gathered was shaken. They were all filled with the Holy Spirit and began speaking God's word with confidence." The language of experience is powerful. When we worship through an experience, the "meeting place shakes." When was the last time your local church hosted a worship experience that was so powerful that the meeting place shook? Today, "shaking" is a metaphor for what it looks like when God softens the hearts of people and causes forgiveness to flow. When visions are revealed and hope is in abundance—this is what happens when we *experience* worship. Having a worship experience is dangerous because God will cause the place to shake. This is why you should consider shifting your language from worship service to worship experience.

If you spend a few minutes searching the websites of local churches across the world, you'll notice a standard contact and worship information template:

- address

- telephone number

- website address

- worship service times and *locations*

I can guarantee you that more than 90 percent of the church websites will list their worship times as "Worship Services" and not "Worship Experiences." At first glance, you may not notice the distinction and may not care about the distinction, but twenty-first-century churches must be focused on the details, especially the difference between worship "service" and "experience." Service by definition means "an act of helpful activity; help; aid."[5] The word *service* is a typical way of describing church that speaks more of a tradition than anything current or relevant or dynamic. It says, "We are here to receive in the same ways we always have, and then to go out into the world to serve." This is not necessarily a negative. It is rooted in good philosophy and theological tradition, and if practiced fully, it can yield positive results. The danger in using the word *service* to describe worship is that it can unintentionally give leaders permission to go lax on worship design. It signals an expectation that we will do things according to a static plan, the same ways over and over again. It doesn't challenge us to think critically, to organize and reorganize the elements of worship, and it doesn't inspire us to pursue innovation. And this is detrimental because a dynamic, changing, responsive, innovative worship experience is necessary to help congregants be empowered and informed to serve the world. When we describe worship as a "service," we can mentally shift the responsibility to God, tradition, and preexisting forms and plans. We can reiterate what's already been done, and call it good. It is certainly more difficult to understand worship as an "experience" and to create worship experiences each week. This requires work, organization, and preparation. It also requires a lot of prayer and teamwork.

When I teach worship design in churches, I explain to the attendees that designing worship is not easy, and this is why many church leaders prefer doing church in a way that is similar to painting by numbers. Very few worship leaders and pastors strategically plan worship on a weekly basis to meet worshippers and elevate them to a new level of awareness. Designing worship is hard. Most worshippers who enter local churches in person or online aren't fully aware that they are receiving the equivalent of day- or weeks-old bread and the church leadership simply warmed up the leftovers of an old song, litany, and sermon and served it on the particular Sunday as if it were fresh. I don't believe leaders are doing this intentionally or maliciously but rather have never been challenged or encouraged to live on a new level of planning and worship experience development. In some cases, this way of doing things results from how clergy are trained by Bible colleges and seminaries. I remember taking a dynamic course on ordering the life of the church through worship, and we students reviewed sermons and worship experiences together as a class. It was a very exciting time in which we welcomed the opinions and thoughts of classmates and helped each other reach our fullest potential. Through no fault of our professors, the one instruction that was lacking from the experience was a reminder to each of us to create this type of learning community once we graduated to help us stay innovative and creative in our weekly, monthly, and annual worship planning. After graduation, we all went to our separate churches, and I doubt many of us repeated the collegial experiences we learned and practiced in Bible college and seminary.

Fast forward a few years after seminary, when I decided to travel a different road to plant a new church. When we gathered a team of twenty-five people to plant Impact Church in January 2007, I knew we were called to Do Church Differently™, and one of the ways we specifically lived out this call was through intentional and pragmatic worship planning and design. We even evolved the model that I learned in seminary and invited more voices into the process who helped us dream and innovate to develop even more dynamic worship experiences. We became the Dyson of worship planning and design, pushing the limit and removing the word *service* in exchange for *experience.*

The second language adjustment is using the phrase "church family" less during worship. The phrase may typically be used by a worship leader, liturgist, worship facilitator, or pastor. Before you frown anymore, there is nothing wrong with the phrase "church family," but if you want to reach more people in the twenty-first-century world, I would use the phrase less and less.

In the Church world there is closed and open language that often positively or negatively impacts a person's experience in your local church during worship. Closed language uses words that create barriers and a lack of flow and understanding. Open language is uses words that are clear and inviting and that create understanding and connection. Typically, when people stand in a worship experience and say "Welcome, church family" or "We are all here," these words and phrases are examples of closed language and may subliminally say "We currently have all of the people and support we will ever need, and if you are visiting, 'Hello,' but we don't need you." One opportunity is to have a small group of your leaders attend worship with a list of closed words and indicate the number of times these words are shared audibly or shown on screens and share the results with the entire leadership team. You may be surprised at the number of times you may be telling new people, "Good to see you, but you really aren't welcome, needed, or included here."

Examples of Closed Words and Phrases

- no
- don't
- family
- church family
- our tradition
- Please see [name of person] to volunteer.

- "We have always done it this way" or "This is what we do each year."

- Meet in the XXXX Room, or the YYYY Hall, or the ZZZZ Parlor.

- acronyms of any kind: EBC Ministry or YXZ Fund

- denominational language or names of denominational groups of any kind: "You are invited to our denominations, annual Family Revival."

Remember to always consider your use of langauge and ensure the language is open rather than closed. Making these adjustments is the fastest and cheapest way to develop a culture of worship design.

II. Productization

"Productization" is the process of analyzing the needs of present and potential customers in order to design products or services that will satisfy their needs. One of the best examples of this is the app world of technology design. I remember watching one of the band members from our church tuning his instrument by using his smartphone. This is an example of how tech companies develop products that help customers achieve their goals and optimize their personal and professional talents. After seeing this, I immediately inquired how this worked, and he said he was using an app. I was thrilled and thought, "Wow! What if the church developed resources for congregants before they even knew they needed the resource?" In the technology business, companies can't wait for a need before they create a product; they have to develop the product in advance of the need and create a demand. It is a way of thinking and development that is often foreign to local churches, and many local churches are behind the eight ball and are left to be second adapters of technology and design, especially as it relates to worship. So what does this have to do with worship? Developing a mind-set of "productization" in our churches can push worship and worship design to the next level. Over the past ten years, more and more resources are entering the marketplace that make it easier for churches to innovate worship and worship design. Just think that more than ten years ago, these products weren't even available, and now we see cutting-edge worship leaders and technology companies developing and innovating software and resources that aid our local churches in reaching people in new and creative ways.

As we keep with the theme of the two previous scriptures from Acts for this chapter, there is a story about the Day of Pentecost, when the Holy Spirit indwelled in the people who would go on to start the early Christian Church, "When Pentecost Day arrived, they were all together in one place. Suddenly a sound from heaven like the howling of a fierce wind filled the entire house where they were sitting. They saw what seemed to be individual flames of fire alighting on each one of them. They were all filled with the Holy Spirit and began to speak in other languages as the Spirit enabled them to speak" (Acts 2:1-4). This presents a powerful reflection of what happens when we allow God's spirit to fall afresh upon each of us and fill us with new thought and purpose. The Church has a leg up on the business world in that we operate with a new spirit and power that enables us to discern God's will and innovate systems and processes that bless God's kingdom. The disappointing news is that we don't always utilize these gifts, and in most cases, we fall behind culture and become lagging indicators and not leading indicators of the greatness of God in our world.

Productization is a mind-set that has to be captured as we embrace God's spirit within and follow the Acts 2 model, and as we partner together with like-minded leaders to innovate worship to another level. Notice that Acts 2 says that the Christ followers were together. Whenever we plan worship in a silo, absent community, we miss the essential ingredient of growing together in faith and challenging one another to reach existing and new people through worship by design. We will talk more about this in the section that addresses worship planning, but we must also be reminded that we often plan worship absent of the Holy Spirit as well. I know you are thinking, "The Holy Spirit is always present," and you are correct, but the presence of the Holy Spirit and welcoming the Holy Spirit into your worship planning space and process are two different things.

Let's go back to the example of the musician tuning his instrument with his smartphone by using an app. Just a few years ago, no one would have believed it would have been possible to tune an instrument with a smartphone, but a few individuals on a research and development tech team pushed the limits and created a resource for musicians that is invaluable. Are you creating worship for attendees that is so valuable that they can't live without it? If your answer is no, you need this chapter, but more important, you need to develop a discipline of productization with those who help plan worship in your local church and make it a high priority.

Ask a simple value proposition question related to worship productization is, "Is worship in our faith community valuable?" When our church was worshipping in a local middle school in a particular community, we saw alarming data related to HIV/

AIDS rates in our immediate geography. If you are like the de-nomination we are affiliated with, there are no 1-2-3 solutions, rule guides, or books of worship that speak directly to this kind of contextual data. This is where productization comes into play, and you partner with people and the Holy Spirit to create worship that is valuable to people. Our solution was to have a free HIV/AIDS testing session during worship. Of course, some people thought we were crazy, but like the R&D people who created the app for tuning instruments, we knew people in our worship com-munity needed a solution to and awareness of the health concerns that were around them. Our hunch worked, and the Sunday was amazingly successful, with a large number of people getting tested and empowered by knowing their status. We added value to our worship experience and to those attending. That is worship design productization 101.

III. Planning

Some pastors and other leaders feel worship should be 100 percent spontaneous and in the moment. I am not knocking spontaneous and in-the-moment worship, but I am recommend-ing putting thought into planning before you present what God has placed on your heart to the people. Worship is more than what happens on the chancel or stage during a particular time frame. Thus, all aspects of the attendees' worship experience, from the time someone drives on the lot until the time they leave, should be planned. I enjoy quick-service restaurants, and I admit I spend way too much time at many of them, but the ones I like the most plan for their customers the best. I remember touring the corpo-rate offices of one of my favorite quick-service restaurants, and I was blown away to see an actual full-scale restaurant inside their corporate building. The purpose of the full-scale restaurant was to ensure all team members could adequately plan meals and services for their customers, and what better way to do it than in a full-scale restaurant? This quick-service restaurant knew that if team members planned and practiced in a mock restaurant, then when they were in a real-life situation with customers, their chance of success would be high and customer ratings would be positive. Wouldn't planning and practice bring a positive outcome?

One of the ways we plan for worship by design at our church is to gather a team of insiders/outsiders to help think, create, and innovate worship. Remember the Dyson company quote on how they put so much energy back into developing products? The same is true for your local church. You need three types of people in your worship-planning meetings: How People, Why Not People, and When People.

How People

The how people are analysts by nature and need all of the non-emotional information up front; they need to know if the plan for the meeting is to focus on Christmas, Easter, first quarter, and so forth. They ask why are we here and what are we doing? Really tactical and non-emotional questions. These are people who ask the "How" questions such as: How are we going to find this prop? How are we going to rehearse this song in one week? How are we going to get real animals for the manger scene for the Christmas Eve worship? Remember, their questions aren't meant to block the road of innovation but to clear it through clarification for easier passage.

These individuals may not be the most creative, but they keep the meeting focused and help develop a productive outcome.

Without these people, the Why Not People (Creatives) will hijack the meeting and spend two hours eating food and laughing. Typically, the "how" people may be the best facilitators for the worship-planning meeting because they will keep everyone else on track.

Why Not People

As I just mentioned, the Why Not People are the creatives, who are necessary because they are always pushing the envelope and asking, "Why can't we have an actual plane in the parking lot?" or "Why can't we turn the stage or pulpit into a real swimming pool?" This is the way creatives think, and without creatives, the world would have more money in the bank but would be a very boring place to live. These are the people who ask additional "Why" questions, such as: Why are you limiting my creativity? Why do we only have twenty minutes allotted for ideation on our meeting agenda? Why can't we have more time and resources to dream big? These are people who dream for fun and will keep the room and discussion lively with fresh and creative ideas for worship. You need creatives on the planning team because without them worship will be static and will never reach new people who are seeking something fresh and creative.

When People

The third group that you need is When People. These people focus on the plan's execution, and they trust the analytical people's questions have been answered, the creatives have been satisfied, and now they want to see a blueprint and begin executing the plan. These individuals are necessary because without them, the plan for worship would never happen; instead it would spin into orbit and never be grounded on a Wednesday, Saturday, or Sunday experience. These are people who don't ask the "how" or "why" questions but the "when" questions such as, "When do you need me to get thirty volunteers for a Saturday morning? When do you need all of the instruments on the stage/pulpit area repositioned for the band? When do you need the outside of the church building to glow with LED lights?" When People are essential on a worship planning team.

As a leader, I have had difficulties trying to manage and talk to each of these types of people in a single meeting setting and keeping everyone on task. Over time, I have learned how to work with them and value their unique abilities and contributions to the team. One of the reasons I wrote the book *Leadership Directions from Moses* was to address the "Difficult Conversations"[6] we have to have as leaders on the journey to achieving the vision. And worship planning gatherings are not immune to difficult conversations. As you lead and facilitate worship-planning meetings, you will have to get used to managing diversity and having difficult conversations from time to time. When I was new to facilitating worship-planning meetings, I wanted everyone to be of one accord and participate in the entire experience. But I later learned this was my naive idea. People have to participate in the areas where they are going to add the most value and not simply act as place holders.

Let's go back to the three categories: How People, Why Not People, and When People. Each is essential for planning and executing excellent worship by design. While evaluating the worship-design team, determine if you have one or two people in each of these categories, and if not, you know your starting point is to recruit these persons from within your church or outside your church. I found some of the best worship planning team member support from people who did not attend our church and had skills in programming, design, creativity and writing that were essential to our planning processes. As you build diverse teams, the group diversity may seem challenging at times but in the end will be a blessing. Remember that the meeting location for the worship-planning meeting is vital to the process as well. Make every attempt to plan worship outside of your church and meet in a place that is creative, filled with people, loud or noisy, and reminds participants of the people your church currently isn't reaching.

Churches often make the mistake of planning worship inside their four walls and, without any ill intent and consequently plan worship for the people they currently see and not those they hope to see. This is called Country Club worship planning or Members Only worship planning. The twenty-first-century vital and growing church plans worship in community to help absorb the needs of those around them, challenge themselves to plan worship on another level, and communicate with people who are out of their loop. There are times when I work on my sermons or meet with people in restaurants, coffee shops, and general marketplaces, and it never fails that I overhear a conversation that confirms a sermon idea I've had or decision I've made, or gives me a new thought about everyday life that I never considered. It makes my sermon and meeting even better. Once, in the early stages of planning worship in public places, our finance team had a significant meeting in a local bar/pub where we made a huge financial faith move. As we were leaving the bar/pub, we met a person who attended Impact while living in Georgia, and when on work assignment in Florida, he attended another church. He commented on some of the things his Florida church was doing that were in direct alignment with the big financial faith decision we just made around a table and appetizers. Wow! I thought to myself, "If we had held the meeting behind our comfortable church walls, we would have never received such a great confirmation." I encourage you to take all of your meetings outside your church walls and see how quickly your teams are inspired and evolve.

As you can see, there are many reasons why the best place to host a worship-planning meeting is outside of your local church, meeting in the community where the people live whom you are not currently reaching and would like to reach. I know this sounds odd, but many local churches aren't thriving because they are not thinking outreach through worship. Instead, they are thinking in-reach, and consequently have become country clubs for Jesus Christ. Even now as I am writing this chapter, I am in a local restaurant with the community I hope to reach and inspire and remaining open to the community to reach and inspire me as well. I become a better leader when I am in community and inspired to be different and grow.

One of the final steps to worship planning after you have the right people and right meeting space is to have food. I can hear you saying in your mind, "He has no idea how limited our budget is" or "We have no budget, and he is asking us to spend money on food." I hear you loud and clear, but remember most churches are led by volunteers, and the volunteers who attend your worship-planning gatherings will be donating their time after a full day of work or other activity. Many of these volunteers can only attend if they bring their kids, so it is always a plus to provide food because the funds you spend for food will be returned a hundred-fold. Trust me, it is worth a few appetizers, hot dogs, hamburgers, sodas, and bottles of water.

After you have the right people, right place, and right food, find the right facilitator to lead you through this very simple meeting schedule:

A. Say Thank You and Pray

B. Ice-Breaker or Hello My Name Is and I....

C. Today Our Focus Is Easter (Example Only)

D. Break into Three Teams, Ideate, and Discuss:

    Team 1. Easter Theme and Budget

        (Theme Approach to Easter and Money and In-Kind Donations Needed)

    Team 2. Easter Outside

        (Everything Outside the Walls: Parking, External Aesthetics, Etc.)

    Team 3. Easter Inside

        (Everything Inside the Walls: Greeters, Ushers, Worship Order, Music, Etc.)

E. Teams Meet for 30–45 Minutes, Reconvene, and Put All Ideas on the Wall (Spaghetti)

F. Take a Vote or Get Consensus to Narrow Down Theme, Outside and Inside Amenities

G. Conclude the Meeting by Saying Thank You, Assigning Follow-up Tasks, and Deciding on Next Meeting Date

IV. Execution

Execution is all about implementing the worship design plan. If the plan has been properly developed and practiced, execution will take place with limited difficulties. Even though there will always be things that come up, you and your team can handle those as they surface. A really essential pre-step to execution is practice and ensuring your team has runway to practice the big experience like Easter before Easter Sunday. Winging it is not a good plan or practice approach if you want to reach existing and new people. In our church, we make it a point to arrive at least one hour before worship and have each person sharing in worship practice his or her part so we have excellent execution. In the case of Easter or Christmas, we practice before the actual day of the worship experience to ensure excellent execution. As you are executing the plan, try not to do major course corrections or make critiques because it will deflate the energy of the team. These corrections should have been seen and addressed during practice. Any additional corrections need to be saved for the evaluation time.

V. Evaluation

Evaluate the results with your worship-planning team after the worship experience, program, or event. Try not to make the mistake I made and begin the evaluation session with critique, but rather, begin the evaluation session with celebration and give each person an opportunity to celebrate a team win and a personal win. Trust me, this will go a long way and help you develop as a leader and develop other leaders. People are people, and mistakes will happen, and you won't win the game every time. It is most important to remember that if the worship participants felt the grace of Christ and had a great time doing it, it's a win. A great opportunity for the evaluation session is to select a facilitator for the session who does a really good job focusing on the positive and not the negative. Having the right facilitator for the evaluation sessions will encourage your team and position them to do an even greater job the next time.

You are in the right position to begin a worship design process or enhance your current worship design process. Keep language, productization, planning, execution, and evaluation in view and know that through the power of the Holy Spirit, great team members, and commitment to planning you will reach new people for Jesus Christ and retain the people who are currently committed to Jesus Christ.

Smart Church Reflection

Reclaim

Worship is one of our greatest expressions of God's grace in our lives, and it is troubling when churches limit their worship to a service and not an experience. Reclaim the gift of God through worship that God has placed in you, develop a team, and trust the guidance of the Holy Spirit.

Rethink

Worship is powerful and should never be boxed in to fit the expectations of people or denominations. You have an ability to think as it relates to designing worship. Don't be afraid to trust God for a new recipe to reach new people through worship by design.

Regenerate

If you are specializing in non-design worship, shift to design worship that speaks to the soul and context of the people you wish to reach. Trust God to meet you in your planning and execution process.

Chapter 5

SYSTEMS

I n the closing chapters of *Zero to 80*, which our team wrote a few years ago, we offered the following wisdom, "Whether we are planting new churches or leading existing churches, we have to do the hard work of re-visioning our system to give people the freedom to focus on the mission side of the goal and not the maintenance side of the goal."[1] When our team wrote these words, our church was just a few years old with much fewer people than we have now, and the words we wrote years ago continue to hold us accountable to systems development today. We joked as a team in the early days when we said, "Each quarter we experience a shift in one area in our church and we have to constantly adjust." From quarter to quarter we would have to change volunteer leaders in particular areas, curriculum for small groups, processes for vendor payment, procedures for worship readiness, and even alarm codes for entry into our office spaces. The list of changes over the years has been exhausting, and there has never been a period when we said, "Okay, the current system or process will last us forever." In church health and growth, whenever you cease to change and evolve, you are no longer reaching new people and the people who are currently with you are no longer growing. Perhaps it is because I grew up in Texas in driving distance to the Space Center that as a child I became deeply fascinated with space and space travel. I love to watch television series on space travel and become glued to the television when I see how far our exploration in space has come over the last sixty years. Who would have ever imagined that people would be living in outer space on a space station and we would one day be close to sending people to Mars. Wow! Amazing! The systems designs in the early space shuttles for their time were cutting-edge and beyond anything anyone could ever imagine. Some of the best scientists and engineers packaged and developed technology to allow human beings to travel further and higher than any commercial jet. In many cases, the space industry had to invent certain types of technology to bring about the vision of space travel, and they refused to allow a lack of resources or limited imaginations to prevent the achievement of the goal of sending people into outer space. In a single space shuttle, there are literally millions of moving parts and systems working together to achieve a common goal of space travel, and although the original space shuttles, decades ago, were created with the latest and greatest technology and systems, today they are dated and obsolete. Astronauts would not consider traveling to outer space in a fifty-year-old space shuttle with dated systems because engineering has evolved at light speed, and the current advancements far outweigh the technology systems of the past.

Similar to space travel, our systems in the local churches where we serve become dated, and if we are not intentional in managing and innovating our systems, we will cease to optimize our ability to make disciples for Jesus Christ. Systems help the world go 'round, and the Church is not immune from the blessing and curse of systems. Depending on your professional background, when you hear the word *systems* you immediately apply it to your professional training and equipment you use to do a great job. But in this case, the word *systems* is more about human behavior than about structures and equipment. The following are three types of systems to consider as you are developing your 4D Smart Church. Focusing intently on these three types of systems in your local church will help your church become more vital and healthier.

People Systems

People systems are at the heart of human behavior, and asking people to adjust or change their behavior is difficult for the leader and the follower. If your church is to be a 4D Smart Church, people will have to be willing to change their behavior and ultimately the way they think about systems in your local church. In his book *Leadership Pain*, Dr. Samuel Chand gives the following formula for growth and change:

Growth = Change
Change = Loss
Loss = Pain
Thus,
Growth = Pain[2]

People systems are difficult to change because in order for growth and health to happen in your church, you have to be willing to ask people to change. And change is very, very, very painful. In your local church, staff team, or organization, your greatest asset is people; your worst headaches and difficulties will be people also. Since the church is made of volunteers, managing people can be more difficult than in a for-profit setting because volunteers aren't paid and their lives take precedence over the needs of the organization or church. Even though this is the case, you can't despair and you have to always look beyond the surface layer to the systems layer and as a leader, fine-tune the system to get a better result. For instance, systems most churches fail to establish with their volunteer leaders are job descriptions, expectations, and metrics. When I was growing up, Mr. Jackson was my Sunday school teacher, and he was a phenomenal teacher who taught me so much about life and God. I will forever be grateful for Mr. Jackson, and I know he is enjoying Heaven. Now, as an adult and pastor who is responsible for leading and guiding key volunteers, I think back to the church where I grew up and Mr. Jackson and wonder if the pastor of the church ever gave Mr. Jackson a job description for being a Sunday school teacher and expressed expectations and metrics with him. Chances are, Mr. Jackson never received these tools as a leader in a local church, and although he did an excellent job as a Sunday school teacher, I wonder how many more students our Sunday school class could have reached if the church had introduced this system. In some cases, especially with volunteers, we assume systems restrict and limit the abilities of leaders, but it is the exact opposite, especially for volunteers. Since volunteers have limited time to serve in our local churches, giving them a description of duties, metrics and expectations is a blessing and frees them up to be successful in alignment with the church's vision and mission. When we fail to give them job descriptions, metrics, and expectations, we leave success to chance, and the likelihood of them getting off task and not meeting the goal is likely. As a leader of a church, I think about volunteers like Mr. Jackson who raised me in local churches during my youth and I will always be grateful for their help and support, and their love for me gives me an even deeper desire to resource the volunteers I work with today in the local church to set them up for success and not failure.

It is vital that we cast a clear vision and expectation with our volunteers and our staff so that we position them for success and help manage their behavior in our settings so the Church wins and people are reached for Jesus Christ. Our church has grown rapidly since 2007, and out of all of the things I was taught in undergraduate majoring in education, and in seminary majoring in theology, I was never taught people systems and how to manage people as it relates to human behavior. If you are like me, you will likely hit your head against the wall a few times before you get it right and then hit your head against the wall again after you get it right. Here are a few lessons I learned as it relates to people systems in the local church.

1. All People Are Worthy, but All People Don't Have the Same Skills and Capacity.

In the hospitality chapter, we focused on people being worthy. I am not undoing that work, but people do have different levels of capacity and skill for certain work. In the Church, we need warm bodies to help, and sometimes, because the workload is so great, you will take any warm body. But in the long run the wrong warm body will do more damage and harm than having no body in the position or role at all. As you are building your team and working toward goals, love and like everyone but always place the right person with the right skill in the right position. If you don't, your church or team will never achieve its goals. Align the right goals and visions with the right people to achieve them. Don't forget the story about my awesome Sunday school teacher Mr. Jackson, and empower leaders like Mr. Jackson with a description of duties, metrics and expectations.

2. People Are People.

When people ask me about the success of our church, what I think to myself the most is, "I wasn't ready for the people side of church." When our core team started Impact Church, our entire staff and volunteer base could fit around a table or two at a local coffee shop. Now we have hundreds of volunteers, more than fifty people on staff, and a multimillion-dollar annual budget. Wow! That's the operational side of growth. Imagine what the spiritual and programmatic sides of growth look like. It has been a whirlwind of a ride, and what I was least prepared for were the people. I know this sounds outlandish because I am a pastor. It is so funny how many church leaders will pray the prayer of Jabez in 1 Chronicles 4:10, "If only you would greatly bless me and increase my territory. May your power go with me to keep me from trouble, so as not to cause me pain." God has granted this request to leaders, and often they are surprised and ill-prepared when people really show up. I believe God answered our Jabez prayer and people showed up, but what I didn't realize is that people bring all of their stuff with them. There have been a number of times as a leader when I have been disappointed with myself and the people around me for various reasons. Sometimes I attempt to have a pity party, but God reminds me about the prayer of Jabez and how I asked for more people. Whenever people show up to attend your church, to serve in your church, or to work in your church, they will bring tremendous gifts and they will also bring tremendous issues that will challenge your patience and the culture of the organization. In these times, remember your feet and their feet are made of clay, and each of you are on the same journey of grace. I have found the best way to manage the people side of church is to have a clear vision, continuosly emphasize that vision of the church, and check with leaders to make sure they are tracking to the vision. Sometimes we create disagreements and conflict because as leaders we aren't clear and expect people to automatically understand and follow the vision.

3. Self-Growth Can't Be Ignored.

John Maxwell lists a law of leadership called the "Law of the Lid" in his book *The 21 Irrefutable Laws of Leadership*. He said, "Leadership ability is always the lid on personal and organizational effectiveness. If the leadership is strong, the lid is high. But if it's not, then the organization is limited."[3] Over my years leading as a pastor and leader in general, the words of John Maxwell and "The Law of the Lid" philosophy encourages and challenges me to be a better and more self-aware leader. If you are a leader and you are leading with a lid, you aren't growing and the people whom you are leading aren't growing very well either.

As a leader, you are controlled by systems of behavior, and sometimes your professional system of managing, leading, and thinking can do harm to the organization because you are managing, leading, and thinking on a level that the organization was on five years ago, and the organization evolved but you didn't. It has also been said that "leaders are learners." If you are no longer learning as a leader, you are creating a people system in your church that will hinder growth and health, not create growth and health. If you are currently in a leadership plateau, consider taking a break and smelling the roses. Travel to other churches and be encouraged by the work of colleagues and see if there is a better way to do the work that is causing you the most anxiety at the moment. Take time with family and friends and unplug from the work of the church and trust God will take care of God's church through a fantastic team who will keep things going. Who knows? The church may operate even better when you are away on break. Finally, find a mentor who will help you see your strengths and opportunities and coach and inspire you to the next level. In the same that way you have to evolve the system of learning for the leaders in your church, you also have to evolve the system of learning for yourself.

One of the constant areas of growth and learning for me as a leader is in the area of faith development. Faith has always been a lid in my life that I struggle to grow to a higher level. When we initially started Impact Church in a middle school, we invested in an audio equipment piece called an audio snake, which allows the audio team to connect to the audio board in one part of the building and run a long single line of cords to the stage area to connect the microphones. Because we were a new church, our funds were limited, and as one of the lead decision makers, I often made decisions based on our current resources and not faith and our future capacity. I was struggling with a leadership lid. I was thinking at a much lower level of capacity than God was taking our church, and when I reflect on those days now, I regret that I did not trust God more and think at a greater level of faith. When the audio team provided three models of audio snakes ranging from cheap to expensive, I chose the cheapest model, which was purchased and placed into operation. Because we were worshipping in a school and not a permanent church building, every piece of audio equipment had to be installed before worship and taken down and removed after worship each Sunday. After a few months of the continual wear and tear on the cheap audio snake, it malfunctioned. We had to purchase a more-expensive snake, and in the end spent more funds in total by going the cheapest route in the beginning. Some leaders would step back from this example and say this is all about finance and equipment, but it is much deeper than that. It is about a system of learning as a leader and how leaders often fail to institute personal systems of growth to address their leadership lids. Most people make decisions based on their current capacity and never take into consideration how their abilities and capacities will grow over time. Therefore, invest in the future now. This is a learned behavior that we have developed over time and can be difficult to break through that mind-set when church leaders are placed into the role of having to make daily key decisions.

As you journey through systems evolution, the most consistent system you will face and have to address and evolve are people. Remember, you are included in the list of people as well.

Open and Closed Systems

Beyond people systems there are also open and closed systems in the local church that can help your local church grow and become healthier. We addressed open and closed systems referring to language in the worship chapter, but let's talk about a more holistic view of open and closed systems in your church beyond worship that are important. Let's take a moment to expound more on open and closed systems that we referred to in the previous chapter on worship. In the worship section we referred to it as open- or closed-language systems such as "church family" or "We are all here." When we talk about open/closed systems in this chapter, it is a little different from language because it reflects a way of thinking or operating for a local church. In the following closed- or open-system diagrams, diagram A is a perfect circle with no entry or exit points, and whatever is inside the circle remains in the circle and whatever is outside the circle remains outside the circle. Diagram B is a perfect circle as well, but it has a dotted-line barrier indicating items can enter and exit the space. The reason some churches don't grow isn't because they don't love God or operate through the power of the Holy Spirit, but rather their entire way of thinking and their systems are designed around diagram A and not diagram B. If you are leading a church that is systematically organized around diagram A, one of your greatest challenges will be to evolve the system around diagram B. In diagram A, your church is insulated and doesn't consider the world outside and likely fights against every good new and innovative evangelistic idea that comes up in a committee or team meeting. If your church is functioning around diagram A, it is likely on the maintenance and preservation life cycle. You will know this because the characteristics of this part of your life cycle include "the ministries [beginning] to focus more on the people who are already connected to the church than the people they are trying to reach…the methods are sacred. The congregation will run any pastor out of town who attempts to change the worship style or the ministry programming."[4] The danger in diagram A systems operation is that leaders get stuck and refuse to change, and if change is delayed too long, the church will ultimately die.

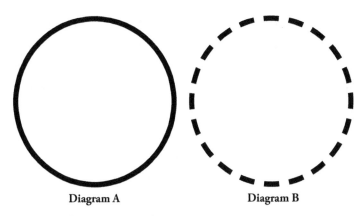

Diagram A   **Diagram B**

If your church is organized systematically around diagram B, your church is fluid and flexible and always in search of creative partnerships to reach new people and willing to make the difficult and painful growth decisions to change. In diagram B, your church is likely in the "momentum growth and strategic growth" life cycle. The characteristics of these cycles include "people [who] start showing up and inviting their friends. New people invite new people. There's a shift from personalities to teams. The entrepreneurial bent is complemented by an awareness that structure and systems need to be established."[5]

There is still hope for your church if it is currently operating through a closed system. But the path to a flourishing church includes the pain referred to by Dr. Chand. One must realize that there can be no true growth and change without pain. As a leader, you have to decide if the pain is worth the potential result before you can decide to shift your church from a closed-system church to an open-system church. I hope you choose the open-system route and know that God will help you manage the pain and change. Some low-hanging fruit areas to consider first when you begin shifting your church from closed to open systems are volunteerism and generosity. Although churches in general struggle with volunteerism, it may not be because people don't want to volunteer but the system used to capture and follow up with volunteers is flawed. From time to time, leaders in our church mention they don't have enough volunteers, and after additional research we discover people signed up to volunteer in their areas, but the follow-up was poor or people wanted to volunteer in their areas and the instructions to sign up weren't clear and there were too many steps involved. In those cases we have to adjust the system as a church and ensure when people volunteer that they receive a follow-up text, call, email, or social media post immediately so that they know and feel our system is not closed but open to them serving. The second area is generosity and how so many churches can only receive two forms of currency: cash and check. This system of generosity is so closed and dated that we would think it should not have to be addressed in a book or talk, but it does because so many churches are trapped in a generosity time capsule. In our local church, during offering time, we express that we have eight ways for people to give that range from cash, check, online, giving apps, and giving kiosks. I teach many church leaders that they miss out on additional income for their churches because they refuse to open their generosity system to receive donations in multiple ways so their parishioners can share their full generosity. We are living in an age when certain generations have never seen a check, and although they have resources to give to local churches, they will never share their generosity via check or cash.

My fourteen-year-old daughter surprised me and my seven-year-old son during grocery shopping as we were discussing the meal selection for the week. She suggested tacos and further suggested that she would cook the tacos and the side dishes. My son and I were elated because we love tacos and quickly placed the items in the basket for purchase and couldn't wait for taco night.

As taco night arrived and my daughter was preparing the tacos and side dishes, I, like any parent, was monitoring from a distance and asking a million questions, with each response I received right from the fourteen-year-olds' handbook: "I got this." As my daughter was preparing to heat up the queso dip, which is arguably one of the best food groups in the world, she couldn't open the glass jar and release the goodness of the queso. She asked me to open the jar of queso and, like any loving father, I gave it a try. Although I wanted to display my super strength, I struggled to open the jar but I pressed through, and the jar slowly opened and we soon had one of the best taco nights of all times. After all of the preparation and gathered ingredients, the one item that almost ruined taco night was a stuck top on a jar of delicious queso.

Like taco night with my children, we are called as leaders in the local church to open our doors wide and gather around the table of goodness and thanksgiving. But even when we have the right ingredients and side dishes, there is always a chance that the meal and gathering will not be all that it can be. The threat to our successful taco night dinner was a simple jar of queso that was difficult to open. But for your church it is a closed system that won't budge and reach the people who are gathered around your church in communities, businesses, places of recreation, fire stations, and schools waiting on you to open your church's jars of goodness and share them with the world. Like opening my jar of queso, switching from closed systems to open systems will be some of the most difficult work you will do, but it is worth it because the goodness on the inside of your church is spectacular. Please don't miss the greatest opportunity your church has to reach new people because of a closed resource in your church or way of thinking in your church that is closed.

Cultural Systems

The final system is cultural, and any established culture that fails to connect to the emergence of a different culture is at risk of dying. I am not saying this is some clarion call to have gigantic Church summits across the globe about cultural diversity. The major work the Church must do around culture is not global but on a local level that is door to door, business to business, and school to school. It is the good old-fashioned evangelism principle of getting to know your neighbors. Once I was riding with one of our pastors and I mentioned a few things about the businesses close to our church campus. The pastor asked me how I knew this information and I thought to myself, "We are called to pastor the community." So many church leaders exist in communities that they don't know and so have very little understanding of the cultural systems and norms around them. We have seen countless numbers of churches that used to be vitally connected in their communities become boarded up or sold to the highest bidder. Whenever churches and church leaders become disinterested or disconnected from the people in their communities, the church will cease to thrive and grow.

Understanding and engaging in culture and cultural systems is not easy, and we can always make the excuse that we don't have time to make the effort to learn, but the reason the Church grew, as recounted in the book of Acts, is because the early apostles were called to serve communities that were filled with culture and cultural systems. Churches that refuse to die or be outdated in the twenty-first century will reorganize on a grassroots level, which will ultimately effect change at the global level. The reorganization is the churches' willingness to get outside and scan the people and the community and get to know the culture and cultural systems around them. In some cases this will be painful because the

Church will realize some of their theology and practices actually offends its nearest neighbors and instead of attracting new people, they are turning people away. It is the uniqueness of the Church that makes it vital, and the need for the Church to be culturally diverse is greater today than ever before.

For years the Church has thought its battles have been against diverse theologies or religious practices among peer congregations, denominations, or diverse faith communities. We now understand that the great majority of the world could not care less about styles of communion, beliefs about baptism, and other major doctrines of the Church. The world has moved on and is paying more attention to the next fashion trend, soft drink flavor, or social media post. The Church has been so busy perfecting and arguing theology among its own practitioners that it has failed to ask the critical question, "How can we make what we believe relevant to a world filled with smartphones, flat screen televisions, and the Internet?" This is the critical question the Church seems to place on the back burner with hopes that the world will somehow be interested in the theological perspectives on Holy Communion such as consubstantiation and transubstantiation, rather than the local news showing the images of an incident that left a young boy dead on the streets near their church building.

As much as we might like to escape the world and the culture, we can't because the world and culture are here to stay. Growing and vital churches will find a way to immerse themselves in culture and reach new people for Jesus Christ. Managing culture and cultural systems is not easy, which is why so many churches and church leaders would rather remain insulated and act as if the world does not exist around them. The only right answer to the question around culture is for churches to participate in complete cultural immersion in their communities and get to know the people and communities they wish and hope to serve. Churches and communities are stronger not when we all agree but when we all know and respect one another in the midst of disagreements. As a pastor, I shouldn't meet my neighbor, business owner, or fire chief for the first time when there is a disaster or tragedy. I am called to have a relationship with these persons before there is an issue in the community. We are called to pastor the people and the communities around us, and this is the key to unlocking and leveraging the cultural systems around and within your church.

Smart Church Reflection

Reclaim
Systems are a part of life and human behavior. Even Christ dealt with systems in government and the temple, and among His disciples and followers. As you follow Christ, know that you can conquer and navigate the systems around you.

Rethink
When it comes to the systems of people—open and closed and cultural—you will have to think differently about everything and know the way you operated as a leader, team, or organization last year, last month, or last week as well as want to be able to sustain and navigate the new systems you face right now and tomorrow.

Regenerate
Instead of seeing systems as a problem or negative, flip your perspective of the systems that surround your church and begin to manage people and yourself better, illuminate all closed systems, and know that in the twenty-first century, cultural diversity is your friend.

Conclusion

ACHIEVING YOUR CHURCH'S 4D NEW MODEL

We end *4D Impact: Smash Barriers Like a Smart Church* with the reprise of the thought of Jurgen Moltmann's hope for a "better church."[1] I believe in your church and you as a leader and that if the principles of technology, hospitality, worship, and systems are applied, your church can remain vital or become a growing and vital faith community. Since we are living in the greatest evangelistic moment of our lifetime, there are no good or great excuses to become Country Club churches but rather churches that engage the world through the grace of God and share the good news.

It is through this good news of a resurrected Christ that Moltmann shared, "We can return, We can begin anew. We can lift our heads out of the mire of self-depreciation. Why? Because freedom approaches wherever God comes. The world is no longer unchangeable but can be transformed. Man is no longer damned in all eternity. The door is opened. It makes sense, therefore, to knock on the still closed door."² Like Moltmann, I believe there is still hope and the Church of Jesus Christ is called to offer the hope to a world in despair and in need of transformation. But this cannot happen if the Church is weak and dying. We represent the life of Christ, and as growing, vital churches 4D Smart Churches, we will be able to share that life with the world.

In addition to Moltmann's theology of hope, another great thought leader, Edwin Friedman, in his work, *A Failure of Nerve*, offered the illustration of a world that is a "seatbelt society," restrained by and filled with fear.³ Many of our churches and church leaders are fearful and get stuck in the past instead of pressing into a new day of transformation. Friedman's statement and observation was very true and very relevant for the state of many of our churches that not only exist in a "seatbelt society" but are trapped behind barriers that prevent them from being all God created them to be. As a twenty-first-century leader leading a twenty-first-century church, you have to cast fear aside. This will not be easy. Most days as a leader, I lead with fear, but thanks be to God, my faith constantly fights with my fear, and faith wins. As a 4D Smart Church leader, you will have to conquer your fears and die to yourself daily, knowing and trusting that God is keeping and guiding you. I hope like Moltmann and Friedman that the world and the Church will be better and bolder in our present age.

I wrote this book because I believe we are living in the greatest evangelistic age of our lifetime, and we are going to miss all it offers if we, as church leaders, hide behind the barriers and fear of the unknown. Although I have achieved what many would call success in the local church, I have also experienced many failures, mishaps, and struggles in my work in the local church. However,

I still have the faith and belief that we can be a smarter church that breaks and destroys barriers. I am a church practitioner who has tested the 4D waters of Technology, Hospitality, Worship, and Systems, and I believe that if these are implemented in your local churches, you will see excellent results, and, most important, you will see more people choosing to become disciples for Jesus Christ. There can be no greater win than to be connected to Christ through a local church that cares.

I wish you the best, and Godspeed on your 4D Smart Church journey.

NOTES

Introduction

1. Chris Isidore, "Amazon Didn't Kill Toys 'R' Us. Here's What Did," CNN Money, March 15, 2018, https://money.cnn.com/2018/03/15/news/companies/toys-r-us-closing-blame/index.html.

2. Jürgen Moltmann, *The Gospel of Liberation* (Waco, TX: Word, 1973), 12.

1. Your Church's 4D New Normal

1. Peter Beinart, "Breaking Faith," *Atlantic*, April 2017, https://www.theatlantic.com/magazine/archive/2017/04/breaking-faith/517785/.

2. Technology

1. Avi Barel, "Your Smartphone vs. Your PC," Medium.com, August 14, 2017, https://medium.com/adventures-in-consumer-technology/smartphones-will-replace-pcs-soon-541b5c8a4f48.

2. Tony Morgan, *The Unstuck Church: Equipping Churches to Experience Sustained Health* (Nashville: Thomas Nelson, 2017), 2.

3. Olu Brown, 2006 Impact vision statement, "Technology Overview."

3. Hospitality

1. Henri Nouwen, *With Open Hands* (Notre Dame, IN: Ave Maria Press, 2006), 97.

2. Carl Buehner, quoted in Robert W. Shoemaker Jr., "Talking Points: Tips for the Savvy Speechmaker," *Rotarian* (January 1996): 15.

3. Emma Lazarus, "The New Colossus," in *Emma Lazarus: Selected Poems and Other Writings*, ed. Gregory Eiselein (Peterborough, Ontario: Broadview Press, 2002), 233.

4. Brené Brown, *Braving the Wilderness: The Quest for True Belonging and the Courage to Stand Alone* (New York: Random House, 2017), 74.

5. The Barna Group, "Six Reasons Young Christians Leave Church," September 27, 2011, www.barna.com/research/six-reasons-young-christians-leave-church/.

6. *Martin Luther King Jr., The Martin Luther King, Jr. Companion: Quotations from the Speeches, Essays, and Books* of Martin Luther King, Jr. (New York: St. Martin's Press, 1993), 27.

7. Howard Thurman, *Jesus and the Disinherited* (Boston: Beacon, 1976), 85.

8. Miguel Hernandez, "Your Health, the Environment and Wooden Telephone Poles," *Patch* (blog), December 13, 2012, https://patch.com/new-york/ossining/bp-your-health-the-environment-and-wooden-telephone-poles.

9. "Theme from 'Cheers' (Where Everybody Knows Your Name)," by Gary Portnoy and Judy Hart Angelo, copyright © 1982 by ADDAX Music Co., Inc.

10. "Love's in Need of Love Today," by Stevie Wonder. © 1976 (Renewed 2004) JOBETE MUSIC CO., INC. and BLACK BULL MUSIC c/o EMI APRIL MUSIC INC.

11. Andy Stanley, *Next Generation Leader: Five Essentials for Those Who Will Shape the Future* (Colorado Springs: Multnomah, 2003), 72.

12. Carey Nieuwhof, "7 Disruptive Church Trends That Will Rule 2018," careynieuwhof.com, https://careynieuwhof.com/7 -disruptive-church-trends-that-will-rule-2018/.

4. Worship

1. James Dyson, "Our Story: The Accidental Engineer," James Dyson Foundation website, accessed February 6, 2019, http:// www. jamesdysonfoundation.com/who-we-are/our-story.html.

2. Dyson.com, accessed February 6, 2019, https://www. lb.dyson.com/en-LB/community/aboutdyson.aspx.

3. Lovett H. Weems Jr., "Leading between Memory and Vision," *Leading Ideas,* October 26, 2016, https://www.churchlead ership.com/leading-ideas/leading-between-memory-and-vision/.

4. Rebecca Barnes and Lindy Lowry, "7 Startling Facts: An Up Close Look at Church Attendance in America," *Church Leaders,* April 10, 2018, https://churchleaders.com/pastors/pastor -articles/139575-7-startling-facts-an-up-close-look-at-church -attendance-in-america.html.

5. Dictionary.com , s.v. "service" (noun), accessed February 6, 2019, https://www.dictionary.com/browse/service.

6. Olu Brown, *Leadership Directions from Moses: On the Way to a Promised Land* (Nashville: Abingdon, 2017), 23–44.

5. Systems

1. Olu Brown, *Leadership Directions from Moses: On the Way to a Promised Land* (Nashville: Abingdon, 2017), 212–14.

2. Samuel R. Chand, *Leadership Pain: The Classroom for Growth* (Nashville: Thomas Nelson, 2015), 5.

3. John C. Maxwell, *The 21 Irrefutable Laws of Leadership* (Nashville: Thomas Nelson, 2007), 5.

4. Tony Morgan, *The Unstuck Church: Equipping Churches to Experience Sustained Health* (Nashville: Thomas Nelson, 2017), 7–8.

5. Morgan, *The Unstuck Church*, 7–8.

Conclusion

1. Jurgen Moltmann, *The Gospel of Liberation* (Waco, TX: Word, 1973), 11.

2. Moltmann, *The Gospel of Liberation*, 17.

3. Edwin Friedman, *A Failure of Nerve* (New York: Seabury, 2007), 2–3.

CPSIA information can be obtained
at www.ICGtesting.com
Printed in the USA
LVHW010148020319
609246LV00005B/6